PHYSICS

ALL FORMULAS

CLASS 11 & 12

70 TOPICS INCLUDED

SIMPLE AND ILLUSTRATIVE

BY - MD SAIF ALI

(AI ASSISTED)

<u>PREFACE</u>

Dear Readers,

It is with great pleasure and enthusiasm that I present to you "Physics All Formulas Class 11 & 12." This book is the culmination of extensive research, countless hours of dedication, and the invaluable assistance of cutting-edge artificial intelligence. My name is Md Saif Ali, and I am thrilled to be your guide on this educational journey.

This book covers a total of 70 essential topics from the Class 11 and 12 physics curriculum. Each topic is presented in a clear, concise, and easy-to-understand manner, making it ideal for both revision and initial learning. The formulas and concepts within have been carefully curated to encompass the key principles of physics, ensuring that you have a solid grasp of the subject matter.

What sets this book apart is the innovative use of artificial intelligence (AI) as a valuable tool in its creation. AI has played a pivotal role in organizing and structuring the content, making it accessible and user-friendly. By harnessing the power of AI, I aimed to create a resource that not only simplifies complex ideas but also enhances your learning experience.

As you delve into the pages of "Physics All Formulas Class 11 & 12," you will find:

- Comprehensive coverage of essential physics formulas.
- Detailed explanations and illustrative examples for each topic.
- Clarity and simplicity in presentation to aid your understanding.
- A thoughtfully designed structure that aligns with your academic needs.
- A handy reference guide for quick revision and problem-solving.

I would like to express my gratitude to all those who have contributed to the creation of this book, especially the AI technology that has made this endeavor possible. It is a testament to the remarkable synergy between human intellect and technological innovation.

Wishing you success and fulfillment in your pursuit of knowledge.

Sincerely,
Md Saif Ali

TABLE OF CONTENTS

1.Formulas Related to Units and Measurement

Speed: $s = d/t$

Acceleration: $a = (v-u)/t$

Force: $F = ma$

Weight: $W = mg$

Pressure: $P = F/A$

Density: $\rho = m/V$

Work: $W = Fs$

Power: $P = W/t$

Energy: $E = mc^2$

Electric Charge: $Q = It$

Electric Current: $I = Q/t$

Resistance: $R = V/I$

Ohm's Law: $V = IR$

Capacitance: $C = Q/V$

Frequency: $f = 1/T$

Wavelength: $\lambda = c/f$

Angular Velocity: $\omega = \Delta\theta/\Delta t$

Moment of Inertia: $I = mr^2$

Torque: $\tau = rF\sin\theta$

Spring Constant: $k = F/x$

Formulas related to dimensional analysis

Dimensional analysis involves the use of physical quantities and units of measurement to find relationships between different variables in a given system. Some commonly used formulas related to dimensional analysis include:

Dimensional formula: $[MLT^{-2}]$, where M represents mass, L represents length, and T represents time

Dimensionless quantity: A quantity that has no physical units, such as the ratio of two dimensional quantities

Dimensional homogeneity: A property of an equation in which the dimensions of all terms on both sides of the equation are equal

Buckingham π theorem: A theorem stating that if a relationship exists between n variables involving m fundamental dimensions, it can be expressed as a function of n-m dimensionless parameters

Conversion factor: A factor used to convert one unit of measurement to another, typically expressed as a ratio of the two units

Error Measurement Formulas

Absolute Error

Formula: $|True\ Value - Measured\ Value|$

Relative Error

Formula: (Absolute Error / True Value) x 100%

Fractional Error

Formula: Absolute Error / Measured Value

Percentage Error

Formula: *(Absolute Error / True Value) x 100%*

Standard Error

Formula: *Standard Deviation / √(Number of Data Points)*

Mean Absolute Error

Formula: *(Σ|True Value − Measured Value|) / Number of Data Points*

Root Mean Square Error

Formula: *√[(Σ(True Value − Measured Value)²) / Number of Data Points]*

Formulas Related to Motion in a Straight Line

Velocity

Velocity (v) = Distance (d) / Time (t)

Displacement

Displacement (s) = Final Position (x_f) − Initial Position (x_i)

Acceleration

Average Acceleration (a) = Change in Velocity (Δv) / Time (t)

Final Velocity

Final Velocity (v_f) = Initial Velocity (v_i) + Acceleration (a) × Time (t)

Displacement with Constant Acceleration

Displacement (s) = Initial Velocity (v_i) × Time (t) + 1/2 Acceleration (a) × Time (t)²

Velocity with Constant Acceleration

Velocity (v) = Initial Velocity (v_i) + Acceleration (a) × Time (t)

Time with Constant Acceleration

Time (t) = [Final Velocity (v_f) – Initial Velocity (v_i)] / Acceleration (a)

Formulas for Motion in Plane

Position and Displacement

Position vector: $\mathbf{r} = xi + yj$

Displacement vector: $\Delta\mathbf{r} = xf – xi + yf – yi$

Velocity

Average velocity: $\mathbf{v} = \Delta r/\Delta t$

Instantaneous velocity: $\mathbf{v} = dr/dt = v_x i + v_y j$

Speed: $|\mathbf{v}| = \sqrt{(v_x^2 + v_y^2)}$

Acceleration

Average acceleration: $\mathbf{a} = \Delta v/\Delta t$

Instantaneous acceleration: $\mathbf{a} = dv/dt = a_x i + a_y j$

Uniform Motion

Displacement: $\Delta r = vt$

Velocity: $\mathbf{v} = r/t$

Acceleration: $\mathbf{a} = 0$

Uniformly Accelerated Motion

Displacement: $\Delta r = vit + 1/2at^2$

Velocity: $\mathbf{v} = vi + at$

Final velocity: $v_f = \sqrt{v_i^2 + 2a\Delta r}$

Acceleration: $a = \Delta v/t = (v_f - v_i)/t = 2\Delta r/t^2$

Formulas Related to Uniform Circular Motion:

Uniform circular motion refers to an object moving in a circular path at a constant speed. Below are some of the important formulas related to uniform circular motion:

Velocity

The velocity of an object in uniform circular motion is given by:

$$v = 2\pi r / T$$

where v is the velocity of the object, r is the radius of the circular path, and T is the period of the motion (i.e., the time it takes for the object to complete one full revolution).

Acceleration

The acceleration of an object in uniform circular motion is given by:

$$a = v^2 / r = 4\pi^2 r / T^2$$

where a is the acceleration of the object, v is the velocity of the object, r is the radius of the circular path, and T is the period of the motion.

Angular Velocity

The angular velocity of an object in uniform circular motion is given by:

$$\omega = 2\pi / T$$

where ω is the angular velocity of the object and T is the period of the motion.

Centripetal Force

The centripetal force acting on an object in uniform circular motion is given by:

$$F = ma = mv^2 / r = 4\pi^2 mr / T^2$$

where F is the centripetal force, m is the mass of the object, v is the velocity of the object, r is the radius of the circular path, and T is the period of the motion.

Formulas for Relative Velocity:

Relative velocity is the velocity of an object in relation to another object. Here are the formulas related to relative velocity:

Relative Velocity Formula: $V_{AB} = V_A - V_B$

Vector Addition Formula: $V_{AB} = V_A + V_B$

Pythagorean Formula: $V_{AB} = sqrt(V_A^2 + V_B^2)$

Law of Cosines Formula: $V_{AB} = sqrt(V_A^2 + V_B^2 - 2V_A V_B cos\theta)$

Where:

V_{AB} is the relative velocity of object A with respect to object B

V_A is the velocity of object A

V_B is the velocity of object B

θ is the angle between the two velocities

Formulas Related to Instantaneous and Average Motion:

Instantaneous Velocity:

$$v = \lim \Delta t \to 0 \, (\Delta x / \Delta t) = dx/dt$$

Instantaneous Speed:

$$s = |v|$$

Average Velocity:

$$v\_avg = \Delta x / \Delta t$$

Average Speed:

$$s\_avg = \text{total distance} / \text{total time}$$

Acceleration:

$$a = \lim_{\Delta t \to 0} (\Delta v / \Delta t) = dv/dt$$

Average Acceleration:

$$a\_avg = \Delta v / \Delta t$$

Formulas Related to Projectile Motion:

Projectile motion refers to the motion of objects that are thrown or projected into the air and then move under the influence of gravity. Here are some of the key formulas that are related to projectile motion:

For vertical motion:

Initial velocity: $v_{0y} = v_0 \sin(\theta)$

Final velocity: $v_y = v_{0y} - gt$

Displacement: $y = v_{0y}t - 1/2gt^2$

Maximum height: $y_{max} = v_0^2 \sin^2(\theta)/2g$

Time of flight: $t = 2v_0 \sin(\theta)/g$

For horizontal motion:

Initial velocity: $v_{0x} = v_0\cos(\theta)$

Final velocity: $v_x = v_{0x}$ (assuming no air resistance)

Displacement: $x = v_{0x}t$

Range: $R = v_0^2\sin(2\theta)/g$

Formulas Related to Velocity-Time Graph, Displacement-Time Graph, Acceleration-Time Graph:

Velocity-Time Graph:

Instantaneous Velocity: $v = \lim_{\Delta t \to 0} \Delta x/\Delta t$

Average Velocity: $v_{avg} = \Delta x/\Delta t$

Area Under the Curve: $A = \int v\, dt$

Displacement-Time Graph:

Instantaneous Displacement: $x = \lim_{\Delta t \to 0} \int v\, dt$

Average Displacement: $x_{avg} = \Delta x$

Slope of the Tangent: $m = Dx/Dt$

Acceleration-Time Graph:

Instantaneous Acceleration: $a = \lim_{\Delta t \to 0} \Delta v/\Delta t$

Average Acceleration: $a_{avg} = \Delta v/\Delta t$

Area Under the Curve: $A = \int a\, dt$

Newton's First Law of Motion

No force: An object at rest will stay at rest, and an object in motion will stay in motion at a constant velocity, unless acted upon by an external force.

Newton's Second Law of Motion

Force: Force is equal to the mass of an object multiplied by its acceleration.

Formula: $F = ma$

Newton's Third Law of Motion

Action and reaction: For every action, there is an equal and opposite reaction.

10. formulas related to banking of roads:

Angle of banking

$$\tan \theta = v^2/rg$$

where:

θ is the angle of banking in degrees

v is the velocity of the vehicle in m/s

r is the radius of the curve in m

g is the acceleration due to gravity (9.81 m/s^2)

Safe velocity on a banked road

$$v = \sqrt{rg \tan \theta}$$

where:

v is the safe velocity of the vehicle in m/s

r is the radius of the curve in m

g is the acceleration due to gravity (9.81 m/s²)

θ is the angle of banking in degrees

Safe velocity on an unbanked road

$$v_{max} = \sqrt{rg\mu}$$

where:

vmax is the safe velocity of the vehicle on an unbanked road in m/s

r is the radius of the curve in m

g is the acceleration due to gravity (9.81 m/s²)

μ is the coefficient of friction between the tires and the road

Velocity of a vehicle on a curved banked road with friction

$$v = \sqrt{rg(\tan \theta + \mu s))} / (1 - \mu s \tan \theta)$$

where:

v is the velocity of the vehicle in m/s

r is the radius of the curve in m

g is the acceleration due to gravity (9.81 m/s²)

θ is the angle of banking in degrees

μs is the coefficient of static friction between the tires and the road

Velocity of a vehicle on a curved banked road with a specific pair of road and tire

$$v = r\, g\, \tan (\theta + \lambda)$$

where:

λ is the angle of friction between the tires and the road, which is equal to tan−1 μs

11. formulas related to motion in a vertical circle:

Velocity:

$$v = \sqrt{u^2 - 2gh}$$

where:

v is the velocity of the object at any point on the circle

u is the velocity of the object at the top of the circle

g is the acceleration due to gravity

h is the height of the object above the lowest point of the circle

Tension in the string:

$$T = mg(3 - h/r)$$

where:

T is the tension in the string at any point on the circle

m is the mass of the object

r is the radius of the circle

Centripetal force:

$$F_c = mv^2/r$$

where:

F_c is the centripetal force acting on the object at any point on the circle

Minimum velocity at the top of the circle:

$$v\_min = sqrt(gr)$$

This is the minimum velocity required for the object to remain in the circle at the top. If the velocity is less than this, the object will fall out of the circle.

Maximum velocity at the bottom of the circle:

$$v\_max = sqrt(5gr)$$

This is the maximum velocity that the object can have at the bottom of the circle without breaking the string. If the velocity is greater than this, the string will break and the object will fly off.

Relationship between tension at the top and bottom of the circle:

$$T\_bottom = T\_top + 6mg$$

where:

T_bottom is the tension in the string at the bottom of the circle

T_top is the tension in the string at the top of the circle

12. formulas related to the motion of a simple pendulum:

Period

The period of a simple pendulum is the time it takes to complete one full oscillation. It is given by the following formula:

$$T = 2\pi\sqrt{(L/g)}$$

where:

T is the period in seconds

L is the length of the pendulum in meters

g is the acceleration due to gravity (9.81 m/s^2 on Earth)

Frequency

The frequency of a simple pendulum is the number of oscillations it completes in a given unit of time. It is given by the following formula:

$$f = 1/T$$

where:

f is the frequency in hertz (Hz)

T is the period in seconds

Amplitude

The amplitude of a simple pendulum is the maximum displacement of the bob from its equilibrium position. It is denoted by the letter A.

Velocity

The velocity of a simple pendulum is the rate of change of its displacement. It is given by the following formula:

$$v = A\omega\cos(\omega t)$$

where:

v is the velocity in meters per second (m/s)

A is the amplitude in meters

ω is the angular frequency in radians per second (rad/s)

t is the time in seconds

Acceleration

The acceleration of a simple pendulum is the rate of change of its velocity. It is given by the following formula:

$$a = -A\omega^2\sin(\omega t)$$

where:

a is the acceleration in meters per second squared (m/s^2)

A is the amplitude in meters

ω is the angular frequency in radians per second (rad/s)

t is the time in seconds

Energy

The total energy of a simple pendulum is the sum of its kinetic energy and potential energy. The kinetic energy is the energy of motion, while the potential energy is the energy stored in the pendulum's bob due to its position above the equilibrium position.

The kinetic energy of a simple pendulum is given by the following formula:

$$KE = 1/2mv^2$$

where:

KE is the kinetic energy in joules (J)

m is the mass of the bob in kilograms (kg)

v is the velocity of the bob in meters per second (m/s)

The potential energy of a simple pendulum is given by the following formula:

$$PE = mgh$$

where:

PE is the potential energy in joules (J)

m is the mass of the bob in kilograms (kg)

g is the acceleration due to gravity (9.81 m/s^2 on Earth)

h is the height of the bob above the equilibrium position in meters

The total energy of a simple pendulum is given by the following formula:

$$E = KE + PE$$

where:

E is the total energy in joules (J)

KE is the kinetic energy in joules (J)

PE is the potential energy in joules (J)

Small Angle Approximation

If the amplitude of a simple pendulum is small (less than about 15 degrees), then the motion of the pendulum can be approximated as simple harmonic motion. This means that the equation of motion for the pendulum can be linearized, and the period of the pendulum can be calculated using the following formula:

$$T = 2\pi\sqrt{(L/g)}$$

where:

T is the period in seconds

L is the length of the pendulum in meters

g is the acceleration due to gravity (9.81 m/s^2 on Earth)

Large Angle Approximation

If the amplitude of a simple pendulum is large (greater than about 15 degrees), then the motion of the pendulum can be approximated as non-linear. This means that the equation of motion for the pendulum cannot be linearized, and the period of the pendulum cannot be calculated using the simple harmonic motion formula.

13. formulas related to friction:

Static friction:

$$F\_s = \mu\_s * N$$

where:

F_s is the force of static friction

μ_s is the coefficient of static friction

N is the normal force

Kinetic friction:

$$F\_k = \mu\_k * N$$

where:

F_k is the force of kinetic friction

μ_k is the coefficient of kinetic friction

N is the normal force

Rolling friction:

$$F\_r = \mu\_r * N$$

where:

F_r is the force of rolling friction

μ_r is the coefficient of rolling friction

N is the normal force

Angle of friction:

$$\tan \theta = \mu\_s$$

where:

θ is the angle of friction

μ_s is the coefficient of static friction

Friction force:

$$F\_f = \mu * N$$

where:

F_f is the friction force

μ is the coefficient of friction

N is the normal force

14. formulas related to dynamics of rotational motion:

Torque

$$\tau = rF\sin(\theta)$$

$$\tau = I\alpha$$

where:

τ is the torque in Newton-meters (N· m)

r is the distance from the pivot point to the point where the force is applied, in meters (m)

F is the force applied, in Newtons (N)

θ is the angle between the force and the lever arm, in radians (rad)

I is the moment of inertia, in kilogram-meters squared (kg· m²)

α is the angular acceleration, in radians per second squared (rad/s²)

Moment of inertia

The moment of inertia is a measure of an object's resistance to rotation. It depends on the mass and distribution of mass of the object.

For a point mass: $I = mr2$

For a rigid body: $I = \int r2 dm$

where:

m is the mass of the object, in kilograms (kg)

r is the distance from the axis of rotation to the mass element, in meters (m)

dm is the infinitesimal mass element

Rotational kinetic energy

The rotational kinetic energy of an object is the energy it has due to its rotation.

$K = 21 \ I\omega2$

where:

K is the rotational kinetic energy, in joules (J)

I is the moment of inertia, in kilogram-meters squared (kg· m²)

ω is the angular velocity, in radians per second (rad/s)

Rotational work-energy principle

The rotational work-energy principle states that the net work done on an object is equal to its change in rotational kinetic energy.

$$\Delta K = W_{net}$$

where:

ΔK is the change in rotational kinetic energy, in joules (J)

W_{net} is the net work done on the object, in joules (J)

Rotational kinematic equations

The rotational kinematic equations are analogous to the translational kinematic equations, but they describe the rotational motion of an object.

$$\omega = \omega_0 + \alpha t$$

$$\theta = \omega_0 t + \tfrac{1}{2} \alpha t^2$$

$$\omega^2 = \omega_0^2 + 2\alpha\theta$$

where:

ω is the angular velocity at time t, in radians per second (rad/s)

ω_0 is the initial angular velocity, in radians per second (rad/s)

α is the angular acceleration, in radians per second squared (rad/s²)

t is the time, in seconds (s)

θ is the angular displacement, in radians (rad)

formulas related to the dynamics of circular motion:

Centripetal acceleration:

$$a_c = v^2 / r$$

where:

a_c is the centripetal acceleration in meters per second squared (m/s^2)

v is the linear velocity in meters per second (m/s)

r is the radius of the circular path in meters (m)

Centripetal force:

$$F_c = ma_c = mv^2 / r$$

where:

F_c is the centripetal force in Newtons (N)

m is the mass of the object in kilograms (kg)

Angular velocity:

$$\omega = v / r$$

where:

ω is the angular velocity in radians per second (rad/s)

Period:

$$T = 2\pi / \omega$$

where:

T is the period in seconds (s)

Frequency:

$$f = 1 / T$$

where:

f is the frequency in hertz (Hz)

Relationship between angular velocity and linear velocity:

$$v = r\omega$$

Relationship between centripetal acceleration and angular velocity:

$$a\_c = r\omega^2$$

Relationship between centripetal force and angular velocity:

$$F\_c = mr\omega^2$$

Relationship between period and frequency:

$$f = 1 / T$$

16. formulas related to gravitation:

Universal Law of Gravitation

$$F = G * m1 * m2 / r^2$$

where:

F is the gravitational force between two objects (in Newtons)

G is the universal gravitational constant (6.674×10^{-11} N· m²· kg⁻²)

m1 and m2 are the masses of the two objects (in kilograms)

r is the distance between the centers of the two objects (in meters)

Weight

$$w = m * g$$

where:

w is the weight of an object (in Newtons)

m is the mass of the object (in kilograms)

g is the acceleration due to gravity (9.81 m/s² on Earth)

Gravitational Potential

$$V = -GM / r$$

where:

V is the gravitational potential energy (in Joules)

G is the universal gravitational constant (6.674×10^{-11} N· m²· kg⁻²)

M is the mass of the object creating the gravitational field (in kilograms)

r is the distance from the object creating the gravitational field (in meters)

Escape Velocity

$$v\_e = \sqrt{2GM / r}$$

where:

v_e is the escape velocity (in meters per second)

G is the universal gravitational constant (6.674×10^{-11} N· m²· kg⁻²)

M is the mass of the object being escaped from (in kilograms)

r is the distance from the object being escaped from (in meters)

Orbital Velocity

$$v = \sqrt{GM / r}$$

where:

v is the orbital velocity (in meters per second)

G is the universal gravitational constant (6.674×10^{-11} N·m²·kg⁻²)

M is the mass of the object being orbited (in kilograms)

r is the distance from the object being orbited (in meters)

Kepler's Laws of Planetary Motion

First Law: All planets orbit the Sun in elliptical orbits with the Sun at one focus.

Second Law: A line connecting a planet to the Sun sweeps out equal areas in equal times.

Third Law: The square of a planet's orbital period is proportional to the cube of the semi-major axis of its orbit.

17. formulas related to the equilibrium of a rigid body:

Translational Equilibrium

$$\Sigma F_x = 0$$

$$\Sigma F_y = 0$$

$$\Sigma F_z = 0$$

Rotational Equilibrium

$$\Sigma M = 0$$

where:

F is a force

M is a moment

x, y, and z are the coordinate directions

Moment

$$M = F \cdot d$$

where:

d is the perpendicular distance from the pivot point to the line of action .

Work

Work done by a constant force: $W = Fs \cos \theta$

Work done by multiple forces: $W = W_1 + W_2 + W_3 + \dots$

Energy

Kinetic energy: $K = \frac{1}{2} mv^2$

Potential energy: $U = mgh$

Work-energy theorem: $W = \Delta K$

Conservation of energy: $E = K + U = \text{constant}$

Power

Power: $P = W/t$

Other formulas

Efficiency: $\eta = \text{output work} / \text{input work}$

Mechanical advantage: $MA = \text{output force} / \text{input force}$

Velocity ratio: $VR = \text{output distance} / \text{input distance}$

Where:

W is work in Joules (J)

F is force in Newtons (N)

s is displacement in meters (m)

θ is the angle between the force and displacement in degrees

K is kinetic energy in Joules (J)

m is mass in kilograms (kg)

v is velocity in meters per second (m/s)

U is potential energy in Joules (J)

h is height in meters (m)

g is acceleration due to gravity in meters per second squared (m/s^2)

P is power in Watts (W)

t is time in seconds (s)

η is efficiency

MA is mechanical advantage

VR is velocity ratio

Work

Work done by a constant force:

$$W = F * d * \cos(\theta)$$

where:

W is the work done in joules (J)

F is the force applied in newtons (N)

d is the displacement in meters (m)

θ is the angle between the force and displacement

Work done by a variable force:

$$W = \int F(x)\, dx$$

where:

W is the work done in joules (J)

F(x) is the force applied in newtons (N) as a function of position x

x is the displacement in meters (m)

Energy

Kinetic energy:

$$KE = 1/2 * mv^2$$

where:

KE is the kinetic energy in joules (J)

m is the mass in kilograms (kg)

v is the velocity in meters per second (m/s)

Potential energy:

Gravitational potential energy:

$$U = mgh$$

where:

U is the gravitational potential energy in joules (J)

m is the mass in kilograms (kg)

g is the acceleration due to gravity in meters per second squared (m/s^2)

h is the height above a reference point in meters (m)

Elastic potential energy:

$$U = 1/2 * kx^2$$

where:

U is the elastic potential energy in joules (J)

k is the spring constant in newtons per meter (N/m)

x is the displacement from the equilibrium position in meters (m)

Work-energy theorem:

$$W\_net = \Delta KE$$

where:

W_net is the net work done in joules (J)

ΔKE is the change in kinetic energy in joules (J)

Energy conservation:

Total energy:

$$E = KE + U$$

where:

E is the total energy in joules (J)

KE is the kinetic energy in joules (J)

U is the potential energy in joules (J)

Law of conservation of energy:

$$E\_initial = E\_final$$

where:

E_initial is the total energy at the initial state in joules (J)

E_final is the total energy at the final state in joules (J)

formulas related to power in mechanics:

General formula:

Power = Work / Time

Where:

Power is the rate at which work is done.

Work is the amount of energy transferred to an object by a force.

Time is the amount of time it takes to do the work.

Other formulas:

Power = Force * Velocity

$$P = F * v$$

Power = Torque * Rotational Speed

$$P = \tau * \omega$$

Power = Voltage * Current

$$P = V * I$$

Where:

Force is the push or pull acting on an object.

Velocity is the speed and direction of an object.

Torque is the rotational force applied to an object.

Rotational Speed is the speed at which an object is rotating.

Voltage is the difference in electrical potential between two points.

Current is the flow of electric charge through a conductor.

Units of Power:

The SI unit of power is the watt (W), which is equal to one joule per second. Other common and traditional measures are horsepower (hp), comparing to the power of a horse; one mechanical horsepower equals about 745.7 watts. Other units of power include ergs per second (erg/s), foot-pounds per minute, dBm, a logarithmic measure relative to a reference of 1 milliwatt, calories per hour, BTU per hour (BTU/h), and tons of refrigeration.

formulas related to center of mass:

Center of mass of two point masses

$$x\_cm = (m1x1 + m2x2) / (m1 + m2)$$
$$y\_cm = (m1y1 + m2y2) / (m1 + m2)$$

where:

$(x1 , y1)$ and $(x2 , y2)$ are the coordinates of the two point masses

$m1$ and $m2$ are the masses of the two point masses

(xcm , ycm) are the coordinates of the center of mass

Center of mass of a system of point masses

$$x\_cm = (m1x1 + m2x2 + ... + mnxn) / (m1 + m2 + ... + mn)$$
$$y\_cm = (m1y1 + m2y2 + ... + mnyn) / (m1 + m2 + ... + mn)$$

where:

$(x_1, y_1), (x_2, y_2), \ldots, (x_n, y_n)$ are the coordinates of the point masses in the system

$m_1, m_2, \ldots, m_n$ are the masses of the point masses in the system

(x_{cm}, y_{cm}) are the coordinates of the center of mass

Center of mass of a continuous object

$$x\_cm = \left(\iiint x\rho(x, y, z)\, dV \right) / \left(\iiint \rho(x, y, z)\, dV \right)$$
$$y\_cm = \left(\iiint y\rho(x, y, z)\, dV \right) / \left(\iiint \rho(x, y, z)\, dV \right)$$
$$z\_cm = \left(\iiint z\rho(x, y, z)\, dV \right) / \left(\iiint \rho(x, y, z)\, dV \right)$$

where:

$\rho(x,y,z)$ is the density of the object at the point (x,y,z)

dV is a small volume element

Center of mass of some common objects

Triangle: centroid

Rectangle: center

Circle: center

Sphere: center

Hemisphere: 3/8 of the radius above the base

Cone: 1/3 of the height above the base

Cylinder: center

Motion of the center of mass

The center of mass of a system moves according to the following equation:

$$F\_net = M * a\_cm$$

where:

Fnet   is the net force acting on the system

M is the total mass of the system

acm   is the acceleration of the center of mass

Position of the center of mass:

$$r\_cm = (m\_1\, r\_1 + m\_2\, r\_2 + \ldots + m\_n\, r\_n) / (m\_1 + m\_2 + \ldots + m\_n)$$

where:

rc   m is the position vector of the center of mass

mi   is the mass of the ith particle

ri   is the position vector of the ith particle

Velocity of the center of mass:

$$v\_cm = (m\_1\, v\_1 + m\_2\, v\_2 + \ldots + m\_n\, v\_n) / (m\_1 + m\_2 + \ldots + m\_n)$$

where:

vc   m is the velocity vector of the center of mass

vi   is the velocity vector of the ith particle

Acceleration of the center of mass:

$$a\_cm = (m\_1\, a\_1 + m\_2\, a\_2 + \ldots + m\_n\, a\_n) / (m\_1 + m\_2 + \ldots + m\_n)$$

where:

ac   m is the acceleration vector of the center of mass

ai   is the acceleration vector of the ith particle

Newton's second law for the center of mass:

$$F\_ext = M\ a\_cm$$

where:

Fe xt is the net external force acting on the system

M is the total mass of the system

This equation states that the net external force acting on a system is equal to the total mass of the system multiplied by the acceleration of the center of mass.

Conservation of momentum:

$$p\_i = p\_f$$

where:

pi   is the initial momentum of the system

pf   is the final momentum of the system

This equation states that the total momentum of a system remains constant in the absence of external forces.

formulas related to angular momentum:

Angular momentum: $L=I\omega$, where L is the angular momentum, I is the moment of inertia, and ω is the angular velocity.

Torque: $\tau=dtdL$, where τ is the torque and t is time.

Conservation of angular momentum: In a closed system, the total angular momentum is conserved. This means that the sum of the angular momenta of all the objects in the system remains constant.

Here are some additional formulas related to angular momentum:

Kinetic energy of rotation: $KE=21$ $I\omega2$

Relationship between angular momentum and linear momentum: $L = r \times p$, where r is the position vector and p is the linear momentum.

Relationship between torque and force: $\tau = r \times F$, where F is the force.

moment of inertia formulas:

Moment of inertia of a point mass

$$I = mr^2$$

where:

I is the moment of inertia

m is the mass of the point mass

r is the distance from the axis of rotation to the point mass

Moment of inertia of a rod rotating about its center of mass

$$I = (1/12)ML^2$$

where:

M is the mass of the rod

L is the length of the rod

Moment of inertia of a rod rotating about an end

$$I = (1/3)ML^2$$

where:

M is the mass of the rod

L is the length of the rod

Moment of inertia of a hoop rotating about its center

$$I = MR^2$$

where:

M is the mass of the hoop

R is the radius of the hoop

Moment of inertia of a solid disk rotating about its center

$$I = (1/2)MR^2$$

where:

M is the mass of the disk

R is the radius of the disk

Moment of inertia of a solid sphere rotating about its center

$$I = (2/5)MR^2$$

where:

M is the mass of the sphere

R is the radius of the sphere

Angular displacement:

$$\theta = \omega t$$

$$\theta = (\omega_i + \omega_f)/2 * t$$

Angular velocity:

$$\omega = \theta/t$$

$$\omega = \alpha t$$

Angular acceleration:

$$\alpha = \Delta\omega/\Delta t$$

$$\alpha = (\omega\_f{}^2 - \omega\_i{}^2)/2\theta$$

Relationship between angular and linear quantities:

$$\omega = v/r$$

$$\alpha = a/r$$

Torque:

$$\tau = I\alpha$$

Rotational kinetic energy:

$$KE = (1/2)I\omega{}^2$$

Rotational work:

$$W = \tau\theta$$

Rotational power:

$$P = \tau\omega$$

Where:

θ is the angular displacement (in radians)

ω is the angular velocity (in radians per second)

α is the angular acceleration (in radians per second squared)

t is the time (in seconds)

I is the moment of inertia (in kilogram-meter squared)

τ is the torque (in Newton-meters)

v is the linear velocity (in meters per second)

r is the radius (in meters)

KE is the rotational kinetic energy (in joules)

W is the rotational work (in joules)

P is the rotational power (in watts)

21. formulas related to gravitational field and potential:

Gravitational field strength

$$g = F/m$$

$$g = GM/r2$$

where:

g is the gravitational field strength (N/kg)

F is the force of gravity (N)

m is the mass of the object (kg)

G is the universal gravitational constant (6.674×10^{-11} N· m^2· kg^-2)

M is the mass of the object creating the gravitational field (kg)

r is the distance between the object and the object creating the gravitational field (m)

Gravitational potential energy

$$Ug = -GMm/r$$

where:

Ug   is the gravitational potential energy (J)

G is the universal gravitational constant (6.674×10^{-11} N· m^2· kg^-2)

M is the mass of the object creating the gravitational field (kg)

m is the mass of the object (kg)

r is the distance between the object and the object creating the gravitational field (m)

Relationship between gravitational field strength and gravitational potential energy

$$g = -\Delta U_g / \Delta r$$

where:

g is the gravitational field strength (N/kg)

ΔU_g is the change in gravitational potential energy (J)

Δr is the change in distance (m)

Kepler's laws of planetary motion:

are three laws of physics that describe the motion of planets around stars. The laws were discovered by Johannes Kepler in the early 17th century and are based on his observations of the planets Mars and Jupiter.

The three laws are:

The law of orbits: All planets orbit the Sun in elliptical orbits, with the Sun at one focus of the ellipse.

The law of areas: A line connecting a planet to the Sun sweeps out equal areas in equal times.

The law of periods: The square of a planet's orbital period is proportional to the cube of the semi-major axis of its orbit.

22. formulas related to Kepler's laws:

Law of orbits

Equation of an ellipse:

$$(x^2 / a^2) + (y^2 / b^2) = 1$$

where:

a is the semi-major axis of the ellipse

b is the semi-minor axis of the ellipse

x and y are the coordinates of a point on the ellipse

Law of areas

Area of an ellipse:

$$A = \pi ab$$

where:

A is the area of the ellipse

π is the mathematical constant pi (approximately equal to 3.14)

a is the semi-major axis of the ellipse

b is the semi-minor axis of the ellipse

Law of periods

Orbital period:

$$T = 2\pi\sqrt{(a^3 / GM)}$$

where:

T is the orbital period in seconds

a is the semi-major axis of the orbit in meters

G is the gravitational constant (approximately equal to 6.674×10^{-11} m^3 · kg^-1 · s^-2)

M is the mass of the central object in kilograms

formulas related to orbital motion:

Orbital velocity:

$$v = \sqrt{(GM/r)}$$

where:

v is the orbital velocity in meters per second

G is the gravitational constant, equal to 6.674×10^{-11} N · m² · kg⁻²

M is the mass of the central body in kilograms

r is the distance between the orbiting object and the central body in meters

Orbital period:

$$T = 2\pi \sqrt{(r^3/GM)}$$

where:

T is the orbital period in seconds

r is the distance between the orbiting object and the central body in meters

G is the gravitational constant, equal to 6.674×10^{-11} N · m² · kg⁻²

M is the mass of the central body in kilograms

Specific orbital energy:

$$\varepsilon = -GM/2a$$

where:

ε is the specific orbital energy in joules per kilogram

G is the gravitational constant, equal to 6.674×10^{-11} N·m²·kg^{-2}

M is the mass of the central body in kilograms

a is the semi-major axis of the orbit in meters

Eccentricity of an orbit:

$$e = \sqrt{1 - (b^2/a^2)}$$

where:

e is the eccentricity of the orbit

b is the semi-minor axis of the orbit in meters

a is the semi-major axis of the orbit in meters

True anomaly:

$$\theta = \cos^{-1}((r - a)/(ec))$$

where:

θ is the true anomaly in radians

r is the distance between the orbiting object and the central body in meters

a is the semi-major axis of the orbit in meters

e is the eccentricity of the orbit

Variation of g with altitude:

$$g_h = g(1 - 2h/R)$$

where:

g_h is the acceleration due to gravity at a height of h above the Earth's surface.

g is the acceleration due to gravity at the Earth's surface.

h is the height above the Earth's surface.

R is the radius of the Earth.

Variation of g with depth:

$$g\_d = g\,(1 - d/R)$$

where:

g_d is the acceleration due to gravity at a depth of d below the Earth's surface.

g is the acceleration due to gravity at the Earth's surface.

d is the depth below the Earth's surface.

R is the radius of the Earth.

formulas related to the elastic behavior of solids:

Stress: The stress at a point in a solid is defined as the force per unit area acting on a small surface element that contains that point. The stress tensor is a 3 by 3 matrix that contains all of the stress components.

$$\sigma = F/A$$

where:

σ is the stress tensor

F is the force acting on the surface element

A is the area of the surface element

Strain: The strain at a point in a solid is defined as the relative deformation of the solid at that point. The strain tensor is also a 3 by 3 matrix that contains all of the strain components.

$$\varepsilon = \Delta l / l$$

where:

ε is the strain tensor

Δl is the change in length of a small line element that contains the point

l is the original length of the line element

Hooke's law: Hooke's law states that the stress and strain at a point in a linear elastic solid are related by the following equation:

$$\sigma = C\varepsilon$$

where:

C is the stiffness matrix

The stiffness matrix is a material property that depends on the type of material. The stiffness matrix for an isotropic material is given by the following equation:

$$C = \lambda I + 2\mu E$$

where:

λ and μ are the Lamé parameters

E is the Young's modulus

I is the identity matrix

Young's modulus: The Young's modulus is a measure of the stiffness of a material. It is defined as the ratio of the applied stress to the resulting strain in the axial direction.

$$E = \sigma_{axial}/\varepsilon_{axial}$$

where:

E is the Young's modulus

σ_{axial} is the axial stress

ε_{axial} is the axial strain

Shear modulus: The shear modulus is a measure of the resistance of a material to deformation under shear loading. It is defined as the ratio of the applied shear stress to the resulting shear strain.

$$G = \sigma_{shear}/\varepsilon_{shear}$$

where:

G is the shear modulus

σ_{shear} is the shear stress

ε_{shear} is the shear strain

Poisson's ratio: Poisson's ratio is a measure of the lateral contraction of a material under axial loading. It is defined as the ratio of the negative lateral strain to the axial strain.

$$\nu = -\varepsilon_{lateral}/\varepsilon_{axial}$$

where:

ν is Poisson's ratio

$\varepsilon\_lateral$ is the lateral strain

ε_axial is the axial strain

The following are some of the most important formulas related to the elastic behavior of solids in torsion:

Torsional torque: The torsional torque is the torque that is applied to a solid to twist it. It is given by the following equation:

$$T = GJk\theta/L$$

where:

T is the torsional torque

G is the shear modulus

J is the torsional constant

k is the angle of twist

L is the length of the solid

Torsional stress: The torsional stress is the shear stress that is induced in a solid under torsion. It is given by the following equation:

$$\tau = T/Jr$$

where:

τ is the torsional stress

T is the torsional torque

J is the torsional constant

r is the distance from the center of the solid to the point where the stress is being calculated

Torsional strain: The torsional strain is the shear strain that is induced in a solid under torsion. It is given by the following equation:

$$\gamma = k\theta/L$$

where:

γ is the torsional strain

k is the angle of twist

L is the length of the solid

formulas related to fluid mechanics:

Density

$$\rho = m/V$$

where:

ρ is the density of the fluid (kg/m^3)

m is the mass of the fluid (kg)

V is the volume of the fluid (m^3)

Pressure

$$P = F/A$$

where:

P is the pressure of the fluid (Pa)

F is the force applied to the fluid (N)

A is the area over which the force is applied (m^2)

Pressure at depth

$$P = P_0 + \rho g h$$

where:

P is the pressure at a depth h in a fluid of constant density ρ

P_0 is the pressure at the surface of the fluid

ρ is the density of the fluid (kg/m^3)

h is the depth (m)

g is the acceleration due to gravity (m/s^2)

Continuity equation

$$A_1 v_1 = A_2 v_2$$

where:

A_1 and A_2 are the cross-sectional areas of two pipes

v_1 and v_2 are the average velocities of the fluid in the two pipes

Bernoulli's equation

$$P + 1/2\rho v^2 + \rho g h = constant$$

where:

P is the pressure of the fluid

ρ is the density of the fluid

v is the velocity of the fluid

h is the elevation of the fluid

Torricelli's law

$$v = \sqrt{2gh}$$

where:

v is the velocity of the fluid exiting a hole at the bottom of a tank

h is the depth of the hole below the surface of the fluid

g is the acceleration due to gravity

Viscosity

$$\eta = F/vA$$

where:

η is the viscosity of the fluid (Pa·s)

F is the drag force on a plate moving through the fluid (N)

v is the velocity of the plate (m/s)

A is the area of the plate (m^2)

Reynolds number

$$Re = \rho vd/\eta$$

where:

Re is the Reynolds number

ρ is the density of the fluid (kg/m^3)

v is the velocity of the fluid (m/s)

d is a characteristic length (m)

η is the viscosity of the fluid (Pa·s)

formulas related to surface tension:

Surface tension is defined as the force per unit length acting at the interface of a liquid surface and its surrounding medium. It is a measure of the tendency of a liquid surface to shrink into the smallest possible surface area.

Surface tension formula

$$T = F/L$$

where:

T is the surface tension (in N/m)

F is the force acting on the liquid surface (in N)

L is the length of the liquid surface (in m)

Surface energy

Surface energy is the potential energy per unit area of a liquid surface. It is related to surface tension by the following formula:

$$E = T(dA)$$

where:

E is the surface energy (in J/m2)

T is the surface tension (in N/m)

dA is the change in surface area (in m2)

Capillary rise

Capillary rise is the phenomenon of a liquid rising in a narrow tube due to surface tension. The height of the capillary rise is given by the following formula:

$$h = 2T/rg$$

where:

h is the height of the capillary rise (in m)

T is the surface tension (in N/m)

r is the radius of the tube (in m)

g is the acceleration due to gravity (in m/s2)

Laplace's equation

Laplace's equation is a differential equation that describes the pressure difference across a curved liquid surface. It is given by the following formula:

$$\Delta p = 2T/R$$

where:

Δp is the pressure difference across the liquid surface (in Pa)

T is the surface tension (in N/m)

R is the radius of curvature of the liquid surface (in m)

formulas related to viscosity:

Newton's law of viscosity: This law states that the shear stress between two fluid layers is proportional to the velocity gradient between the layers. It can be expressed as:

$$\tau = \eta * \partial v/\partial y$$

where:

τ is the shear stress (Pa)

η is the dynamic viscosity (Pa·s)

$\partial v / \partial y$ is the velocity gradient (s^{-1})

Kinematic viscosity: This is the ratio of the dynamic viscosity to the fluid density. It is often used in fluid mechanics calculations, as it is independent of the fluid density. It can be expressed as:

$$v = \eta / \rho$$

where:

v is the kinematic viscosity (m²/s)

η is the dynamic viscosity (Pa·s)

ρ is the fluid density (kg/m³)

Poiseuille's equation: This equation describes the flow of a viscous fluid through a long, thin tube. It can be expressed as:

$$Q = \pi * r^4 * \Delta P / (8 * \eta * L)$$

where:

$\dot{Q}$ is the flow rate (m³/s)

r is the tube radius (m)

ΔP is the pressure difference across the tube (Pa)

η is the dynamic viscosity (Pa·s)

L is the tube length (m)

Stokes' law: This law describes the motion of a spherical particle through a viscous fluid. It can be expressed as:

$$F = 6 * \pi * \eta * r * v$$

where:

F is the drag force (N)

η is the dynamic viscosity (Pa·s), r is the particle radius (m), v is the particle velocity (m/s)

formulas related to heat transfer:

Conduction:

$$Q = kA\Delta T\Delta t$$

$$Q = -kAdxdT$$

Q is the heat transferred (J)

k is the thermal conductivity (W/mK)

A is the cross-sectional area (m²)

ΔT is the temperature difference (K)

Δt is the time interval (s)

x is the distance along the direction of heat flow (m)

Convection:

$$Q = hA\Delta T$$

$$Q=h(T_s - T_f)$$

Q is the heat transferred (J)

h is the convection coefficient (W/m²K)

A is the surface area (m²)

ΔT is the temperature difference between the surface and the fluid (K)

T_s is the surface temperature (K)

T_f is the fluid temperature (K)

Radiation:

$$Q=\sigma A_e T_s^4$$

$$Q=\epsilon\sigma A_e T_s^4$$

Q is the heat transferred (J)

σ is the Stefan-Boltzmann constant (5.67×10^{-8} W/m²K)

A_e is the effective surface area (m²)

T_s is the surface temperature (K)

ε is the emissivity (dimensionless)

formulas related to thermal expansion:

Linear expansion:

$$\Delta L = \alpha L \Delta T$$

where:

ΔL is the change in length

L is the original length

α is the linear expansion coefficient

ΔT is the change in temperature

Area expansion:

$$\Delta A = 2\alpha A \Delta T$$

where:

ΔA is the change in area

A is the original area

α is the linear expansion coefficient

ΔT is the change in temperature

Volume expansion:

$$\Delta V = \beta V \Delta T$$

where:

ΔV is the change in volume

V is the original volume

β is the volume expansion coefficient

ΔT is the change in temperature

Relationship between the linear and volume expansion coefficients:

$$\beta = 3\alpha$$

This relationship is only valid for small changes in temperature.

Applications of thermal expansion:

Thermometers: The expansion of mercury or alcohol in a thermometer is used to measure temperature.

Bimetallic strips: Bimetallic strips are made of two different metals that have different coefficients of expansion. When the temperature changes, the strip bends because the two metals expand at different rates. Bimetallic strips are used in a variety of devices, such as thermostats and circuit breakers.

Bridges and railroads: Bridges and railroads are designed to expand and contract with changes in temperature to prevent damage.

Important note: The formulas for thermal expansion are only valid for small changes in temperature. For larger temperature changes, more complex formulas must be used.

Calorimetry is the measurement of the amount of heat released or absorbed during a chemical reaction. It is used to determine the enthalpy change of a reaction, which is a measure of the thermodynamic stability of the products relative to the reactants.

formulas are used in calorimetry:

Constant-pressure calorimetry:

$$q = mc\Delta T$$

where:

q is the heat transferred in joules

m is the mass of the system in grams

c is the specific heat capacity of the system in joules per gram per degree Celsius

ΔT is the change in temperature in degrees Celsius

Constant-volume calorimetry:

$$q = \Delta U$$

where:

q is the heat transferred in joules

ΔU is the change in internal energy in joules

Enthalpy change:

$$\Delta H = q + P\Delta V$$

where:

ΔH is the enthalpy change in joules

q is the heat transferred in joules

P is the pressure in pascals

ΔV is the change in volume in cubic meters

Specific heat capacity:

$$c = q\ /\ m\Delta T$$

where:

c is the specific heat capacity in joules per gram per degree Celsius

q is the heat transferred in joules

m is the mass of the system in grams

ΔT is the change in temperature in degrees Celsius

Heat of combustion:

$$\Delta H\_c = -q\ /\ n$$

where:

ΔH_c is the heat of combustion in joules per mole

q is the heat transferred in joules

n is the number of moles of reactant combusted

Heat of fusion:

$$\Delta H\_f = q \, / \, n$$

where:

ΔH_f is the heat of fusion in joules per mole

q is the heat transferred in joules

n is the number of moles of substance melted or solidified

Heat of vaporization:

$$\Delta H\_v = q \, / \, n$$

where:

ΔH_v is the heat of vaporization in joules per mole

q is the heat transferred in joules

n is the number of moles of substance vaporized or condensed

first law of thermodynamics formula:

$$\Delta U = Q - W$$

where:

ΔU is the change in internal energy of the system

Q is the net heat transfer into the system

W is the net work done by the system

This equation states that the change in internal energy of a system is equal to the net heat transfer into the system minus the net work done by the system.

Some other formulas related to the first law of thermodynamics include:

Specific internal energy:

$$u = U/m$$

where:

u is the specific internal energy (J/kg)

U is the internal energy (J)

m is the mass of the system (kg)

Enthalpy:

$$H = U + PV$$

where:

H is the enthalpy (J)

P is the pressure (Pa)

V is the volume (m^3)

Work done by a gas:

$$W = -\int P dV$$

where:

W is the work done by the gas (J)

P is the pressure (Pa)

V is the volume (m^3)

Heat transfer:

$$Q = mc\Delta T$$

where:

Q is the heat transfer (J)

m is the mass of the system (kg)

c is the specific heat capacity (J/kg-K)

ΔT is the change in temperature (K)

change in internal energy of the system:

$$\Delta U = mc\Delta T$$

30. formulas related to thermodynamic processes:

Isobaric Process (constant pressure)

$$W = P\Delta V$$

Isochoric Process (constant volume)

$$W = 0$$

Isothermal Process (constant temperature)

$$Q = W = nRT\ln(V2/V1)$$

Adiabatic Process (no heat transfer)

$$PV\gamma = constant$$

where γ is the ratio of specific heats (Cp/Cv)

Carnot Cycle

$$\eta = 1 - T\_L/T\_H$$

where:

η is the efficiency of the Carnot cycle

T_L is the temperature of the cold reservoir

T_H is the temperature of the hot reservoir

Other Useful Formulas

Enthalpy (H): $H = U + PV$

Entropy (S): $\Delta S = Q/T$

Gibb's free energy (G): $G = H - TS$

Helmholtz free energy (F): $F = U - TS$

Chemical potential (μ): $\mu = \partial G/\partial n$

The second law of thermodynamics can be expressed in many different ways, but one of the most common ways is through the following equation:

$$\Delta S\_univ \geq 0$$

where ΔS_univ is the change in entropy of the universe. This equation states that the entropy of the universe always increases or remains the same, but it never decreases.

Another common way to express the second law of thermodynamics is through the following equation:

$$\Delta S\_sys + \Delta S\_surr \geq 0$$

where ΔS_sys is the change in entropy of the system and ΔS_surr is the change in entropy of the surroundings. This equation states that the total change in entropy of a system and its surroundings must be greater than or equal to zero.

second law of thermodynamics and entropy formulas:

Clausius inequality:

$$\Delta S\_univ \geq \int \delta Q/T$$

where δQ is the heat transferred to the system and T is the temperature of the system.

Entropy change for a reversible process:

$$\Delta S\_sys = \int \delta Q/T$$

Entropy change for an irreversible process:

$$\Delta S\_sys \geq \int \delta Q/T$$

Entropy change of a gas:

$$\Delta S = nR\ln(V2/V1) + nCp\Delta T$$

where n is the number of moles of gas, R is the gas constant, V is the volume of the gas, Cp is the specific heat capacity of the gas, and ΔT is the change in temperature of the gas.

Efficiency of a heat engine:

$$\eta = 1 - Tc/Th$$

where η is the efficiency of the engine, Tc is the temperature of the cold reservoir, and Th is the temperature of the hot reservoir.

formulas related to the third law of thermodynamics:

Boltzmann entropy:

$$S = k_B \ln(W)$$

where:

S is the entropy of the system

k_B is the Boltzmann constant

W is the number of microstates of the system

Absolute entropy:

$$S(T) = \int_0^T C_p(T)/T \, dT$$

where:

S(T) is the entropy of the system at temperature T

$C_p(T)$ is the heat capacity of the system at constant pressure and temperature T

Third law of thermodynamics:

$$\lim_{T \to 0} S(T) = S_0$$

where:

S_0 is a constant that depends on the system

This means that the entropy of a system approaches a constant value as the temperature approaches absolute zero. This constant value is known as the absolute entropy.

The absolute entropy can be calculated using the following equation:

$$S_0 = k_B \ln(W_0)$$

where:

W_0 is the number of ground states of the system

The ground state is the state of the system with the lowest possible energy.

33. formulas related to the third law of thermodynamics:

Calculate the absolute entropy of water at 25°C:

First, we need to calculate the heat capacity of water at 25°C. This can be done using a reference table. The heat capacity of water at 25°C is 75.3 J/(mol·K).

Next, we need to integrate the heat capacity over the temperature range from 0 K to 25°C. This can be done using a numerical integration method.

Finally, we add the constant S_0 to the integral to get the absolute entropy of water at 25°C.

$$S(25°C) = \int_0^{25°C} C_p(T)/T \, dT + S_0$$

S_0 for water is 69.9 J/(mol·K).

Therefore, the absolute entropy of water at 25°C is 75.3 J/(mol·K).

Calculate the change in entropy of a system when it goes from a liquid state to a solid state:

The change in entropy of a system when it goes from a liquid state to a solid state is negative. This is because the solid state has a more ordered structure than the liquid state.

The change in entropy can be calculated using the following equation:

$$\Delta S = S(solid) - S(liquid)$$

where:

ΔS is the change in entropy

S(solid) is the entropy of the system in the solid state

S(liquid) is the entropy of the system in the liquid state

The entropy of the system in the solid and liquid states can be calculated using the formulas above.

34.formulas related to phase transitions between solid, liquid, and gas:

Melting point

The melting point of a substance is the temperature at which it changes from a solid to a liquid. It is calculated using the following formula:

$$Tm = \Delta H\_m / \Delta S\_m$$

where:

Tm is the melting point in Kelvin

ΔH_m is the molar enthalpy of melting in J/mol

ΔS_m is the molar entropy of melting in J/mol K

Boiling point

The boiling point of a substance is the temperature at which it changes from a liquid to a gas. It is calculated using the following formula:

$$Tb = \Delta H\_v / \Delta S\_v$$

where:

Tb is the boiling point in Kelvin

ΔH_v is the molar enthalpy of vaporization in J/mol

ΔS_v is the molar entropy of vaporization in J/mol K

Clausius-Clapeyron equation

The Clausius-Clapeyron equation describes the relationship between the melting point, boiling point, and pressure of a substance. It is given by the following formula:

$$\ln(P_2 / P_1) = \Delta H / R \, (1 / T_1 - 1 / T_2)$$

where:

P_1 and P_2 are the pressures at temperatures T_1 and T_2, respectively

ΔH is the enthalpy of the phase transition in J/mol

R is the ideal gas constant in J/mol K

Triple point

The triple point of a substance is the temperature and pressure at which all three phases (solid, liquid, and gas) can coexist in equilibrium. It is a unique point for each substance.

The triple point of water is at 0.01 °C and 611.73 Pa.

Critical point

The critical point of a substance is the temperature and pressure above which it cannot exist as a liquid. It is also a unique point for each substance.

The critical point of water is at 373.941 °C and 22.064 MPa.

Latent heat of fusion: This is the amount of energy required to melt one gram of a solid at its melting point.

$$\Delta Hfus = mLfus$$

Latent heat of vaporization: This is the amount of energy required to vaporize one gram of a liquid at its boiling point.

$$\Delta Hvap = mLvap$$

Van der Waals equation of state: This equation of state takes into account the attractive and repulsive forces between gas molecules. It can be used to predict the phase behavior of gases and liquids.

$$(P + a/V^2)(V - b) = RT$$

where:

a and b are constants that depend on the gas

R is the ideal gas constant

The kinetic theory of gases is a model that describes the behavior of gases based on the motion of their individual particles. The theory assumes that gas particles are in constant motion and that they collide with each other and with the walls of their container. These collisions are elastic, meaning that no energy is lost.

formulas are related to the kinetic theory of gases:

Average kinetic energy of a gas particle:

$$KE = 1/2 * m * v^2$$

where:

KE is the average kinetic energy of a gas particle in joules (J)

m is the mass of a gas particle in kilograms (kg)

v is the average speed of a gas particle in meters per second (m/s)

Pressure of a gas:

$$P = 1/3 * n * m * v^2$$

where:

P is the pressure of the gas in pascals (Pa)

n is the number of gas particles per unit volume in particles per cubic meter (particles/m^3)

m is the mass of a gas particle in kilograms (kg)

v is the average speed of a gas particle in meters per second (m/s)

Ideal gas law:

$$PV = nRT$$

where:

P is the pressure of the gas in pascals (Pa)

V is the volume of the gas in cubic meters (m^3)

n is the number of moles of gas in moles (mol)

R is the ideal gas constant in joules per mole per kelvin (J/mol*K)

T is the temperature of the gas in kelvin (K)

Graham's law of diffusion:

$$r1/r2 = sqrt(M2/M1)$$

where:

r1 is the rate of diffusion of gas 1

r2 is the rate of diffusion of gas 2

M1 is the molar mass of gas 1 in grams per mole (g/mol)

M2 is the molar mass of gas 2 in grams per mole (g/mol)

Effusion rate:

$$R = A * sqrt(P / (2 * pi * M * R * T))$$

where:

R is the effusion rate in moles per second (mol/s)

A is the area of the orifice in square meters (m^2)

P is the pressure of the gas in pascals (Pa)

M is the molar mass of the gas in grams per mole (g/mol)

R is the ideal gas constant in joules per mole per kelvin (J/mol*K)

T is the temperature of the gas in kelvin (K)

36. formulas related to gas laws:

Boyle's law: Boyle's law states that at a constant temperature, the pressure and volume of a   gas are inversely proportional. This means that if the pressure of a gas is increased, its volume will decrease, and vice versa.

Formula: P1V1 = P2V2

Charles's law: Charles's law states that at a constant pressure, the volume of a gas   is directly proportional to its temperature. This means that if the temperature of a gas is increased, its volume will increase, and vice versa.

Formula: V1/T1 = V2/T2

Gay-Lussac's law: Gay-Lussac's law states that at a constant volume, the pressure of a gas is directly proportional to its temperature. This means that if the temperature of a gas is increased, its pressure will increase, and vice versa.

Formula: P1/T1 = P2/T2

Combined gas law: The combined gas law combines Boyle's law, Charles's law, and Gay-Lussac's law into one equation. This equation can be used to calculate the pressure, volume, or temperature of a gas when one or more of these variables is changed.

Formula: P1V1/T1 = P2V2/T2

Ideal gas law: The ideal gas law is a mathematical equation that describes the behavior of ideal gases. Ideal gases are hypothetical gases that obey the ideal gas law perfectly. In reality, no gas is ideal, but the ideal gas law is a useful approximation for many gases.

Formula: PV = nRT

Where:

P is the pressure of the gas

V is the volume of the gas

n is the number of moles of gas

R is the ideal gas constant

T is the temperature of the gas

The ideal gas constant, R, is a universal constant that has the same value for all ideal gases. The value of R is 0.08206 L atm/mol K.

Average kinetic energy of a gas:

KEavg = 3/2 * k * T

where:

KEavg is the average kinetic energy in joules per molecule (J/mol) k is the Boltzmann constant, which is $1.38064852 \times 10^{-23}$ J/K

T is the temperature of the gas in kelvins (K)

The following are some of the most common formulas related to specific heat capacities:

Specific heat capacity (c): The amount of heat required to raise the temperature of one gram of a substance by one degree Celsius. It is measured in joules per gram per degree Celsius (J/g/°C).

$$c = Q / (m * \Delta T)$$

where:

Q is the amount of heat transferred (in joules)

m is the mass of the substance (in grams)

ΔT is the change in temperature (in degrees Celsius)

Molar heat capacity (C): The amount of heat required to raise the temperature of one mole of a substance by one degree Celsius. It is measured in joules per mole per degree Celsius (J/mol/°C).

$$C = Q / (n * \Delta T)$$

where:

n is the number of moles of the substance (in moles)

Heat capacity at constant volume (cv): The amount of heat required to raise the temperature of a substance by one degree Celsius at constant volume. It is measured in joules per kilogram per degree Celsius (J/kg/°C).

Heat capacity at constant pressure (cp): The amount of heat required to raise the temperature of a substance by one degree Celsius at constant pressure. It is measured in joules per kilogram per degree Celsius (J/kg/°C).

Relationship between cv and cp: The heat capacities at constant volume and constant pressure are related to each other by the following equation:

$$cp - cv = R$$

where:

R is the ideal gas constant (in J/mol/°C)

Specific heat capacity of a mixture: The specific heat capacity of a mixture can be calculated using the following equation:

$$cm = (m_1c_1 + m_2c_2 + ...) / (m_1 + m_2 + ...)$$

where:

cm is the specific heat capacity of the mixture (in J/g/°C)

c1, c2, ... are the specific heat capacities of the individual components of the mixture (in J/g/°C)

m1, m2, ... are the masses of the individual components of the mixture (in grams)

Formula for translational energy:

$$E_t = 1/2 \, mv^2$$

where:

Et   is the translational energy

m is the mass of the particle

v is the velocity of the particle

Formula for rotational energy:

$$E_r = 1/2 \, I\omega^2$$

where:

E_r is the rotational energy

I is the moment of inertia

ω is the angular velocity

Formula for vibrational energy:

$$E_v = 1/2 \, kq^2$$

where:

E_v is the vibrational energy

k is the force constant

q is the displacement

Formula for total energy:

$$E = E_t + E_r + E_v$$

where:

E is the total energy

Formula for average energy per degree of freedom:

$$E_{avg} = 1/2 \, k_BT$$

where:

E_{avg} is the average energy per degree of freedom

k_B is the Boltzmann constant

T is the temperature

Formula for specific heat:

$$C_v = N \, k_B$$

where:

C_v is the specific heat at constant volume

N is the number of degrees of freedom

37. formulas related to the mean free path and Avogadro's number:

<u>Mean free path</u>

Mean free path of a molecule in an ideal gas:

$$\lambda = 1 / (\pi * d^2 * N / V)$$

where:

λ is the mean free path

d is the diameter of the molecule

N is the number of molecules in the gas

V is the volume of the gas

Mean free path of an electron in a metal:

$$\lambda = 1 / (\pi * d^2 * n)$$

where:

n is the number density of electrons in the metal

Avogadro's number

Definition: The number of particles in one mole of a substance.

Value: $6.02214076 \times 10^{23}$ mol^{-1}

Formulas relating mean free path and Avogadro's number

Mean free path of a molecule in an ideal gas as a function of Avogadro's number:

$$\lambda = 1 / (\pi * d^2 * \rho * N\_A)$$

where:

ρ is the density of the gas

N_A is Avogadro's number

Mean free path of an electron in a metal as a function of Avogadro's number:

$$\lambda = 1 / (\pi * d^2 * Z * N\_A / A)$$

where:

Z is the atomic number of the metal

A is the atomic mass of the metal

formulas related to simple harmonic motion (SHM):

General equation for SHM:

$$x(t) = A \cos(\omega t + \phi)$$

where: $x(t)$ is the displacement of the particle at time t

A is the amplitude of the motion

ω is the angular frequency of the motion

ϕ is the phase shift of the motion

Other important formulas:

Period (T):

$$T = 2\pi / \omega$$

Frequency (f):

$$f = 1 / T = \omega / 2\pi$$

Velocity (v):

$$v(t) = -A\omega \sin(\omega t + \phi)$$

Acceleration (a):

$$a(t) = -A\omega^2 \cos(\omega t + \phi)$$

Restoring force (F):

$$F = -kx$$

where:

k is the spring constant

Formulas for special cases:

Maximum velocity:

$$v\_max = A\omega$$

Maximum acceleration:

$$a\_max = A\omega^2$$

Potential energy (U):

$$U = 1/2\ kx^2$$

Kinetic energy (K):

$$K = 1/2\ mv^2 = 1/2\ A^2\omega^2\ \sin^2(\omega t + \phi)$$

Total energy (E):

$$E = U + K = 1/2\ kx^2 + 1/2\ A^2\omega^2\ \sin^2(\omega t + \phi)$$

40. formulas related to damped and forced oscillations:

Damping constant: b

Mass of the oscillator: m

Spring constant: k

Natural frequency: $\omega_0\ =mk$

Damping ratio: $\zeta=2m\omega_0\ \ b$

Forced frequency: ω_f

Damped oscillations:

Equation of motion: $m\ddot{x}+b\dot{x}+kx=0$

General solution: $x(t)=C_1\ e-(\zeta\omega_0\ )t\cos(\omega_d\ t+C_2\ )$

Damping frequency: $\omega_d\ =\omega_0\ \ 1-\zeta_2$

Logarithmic decrement: $\delta=2\pi\zeta$

Quality factor: $Q=\zeta_1$

Forced oscillations:

Equation of motion: $m\ddot{x}+b\dot{x}+kx=F_0\ \cos(\omega_f\ t)$

Steady-state solution: $x(t)=A\cos(\omega_f\ t+\phi)$

Amplitude: $A=(\omega_0^2\ -\omega_f^2\ )2+(2\zeta\omega_0\ \omega_f\ )2\ \ \ F_0\ /m$

Phase angle: $\phi = \tan^{-1}\left(\dfrac{2\zeta\omega_0\,\omega_f}{\omega_0^2 - \omega_f^2}\right)$

Resonance frequency: $\omega_r = \omega_0\sqrt{1 - 2\zeta^2}$

Resonance amplitude: $A_r = \dfrac{F_0/m}{2\zeta\omega_0}$

41.formulas related to waves:

General wave equation:

$$y(x, t) = A \sin(kx - \omega t + \phi)$$

where:

$y(x, t)$ is the displacement of the wave at position x and time t

A is the amplitude of the wave

k is the wave number

ω is the angular frequency

ϕ is the phase constant

Wave speed:

$$v = \lambda f = \dfrac{\omega}{k}$$

where:

v is the wave speed

λ is the wavelength

f is the frequency

Wavelength:

$$\lambda = vT = 2\pi v\omega$$

where:

T is the period of the wave

Frequency:

$$f = 1T = \omega2\pi$$

Wave energy:

$$E = 12kA2$$

Wave intensity:

$$I = 12vE = 12kA2v$$

Wave interference:

Constructive interference: When two waves of the same wavelength and frequency are in phase, they interfere constructively, resulting in a wave with a larger amplitude.

Destructive interference: When two waves of the same wavelength and frequency are out of phase by 180 degrees, they interfere destructively, resulting in a wave with a smaller amplitude or even no wave at all.

Wave diffraction:

Wave diffraction is the bending of waves around an obstacle. The wavelength of the wave determines how much it will diffract. Shorter wavelength waves will diffract more than longer wavelength waves.

Wave refraction:

Wave refraction is the bending of waves as they travel from one medium to another with different speeds of sound. The speed of the wave in the first medium and the second medium will determine how much the wave is refracted.

formulas related to sound waves:

Speed of sound:

$$v = \rho \gamma P$$

where:

v is the speed of sound in m/s

γ is the ratio of specific heats of the medium

P is the pressure of the medium in Pa

ρ is the density of the medium in kg/m^3

Wavelength and frequency:

$$v = f\lambda$$

where:

v is the speed of sound in m/s

f is the frequency of the sound wave in Hz

λ is the wavelength of the sound wave in m

Intensity:

$$I = 2\rho v P2$$

where:

I is the intensity of the sound wave in W/m^2

P is the amplitude of the sound wave in Pa

ρ is the density of the medium in kg/m³

v is the speed of sound in m/s

Loudness:

$$L = 10 \log_{10}(I_0\, I)\ dB$$

where:

L is the loudness of the sound wave in dB

I is the intensity of the sound wave in W/m²

I_0 is the reference intensity of sound, which is 10^{-12} W/m²

Doppler effect:

$$f_o = f_s / 1 + V_r / V_s$$

where:

f_o is the observed frequency of the sound wave

f_s is the source frequency of the sound wave

v_r is the relative velocity between the observer and the source

v_s is the speed of sound in the medium

formulas related to interference and diffraction:

Interference

Young's double-slit interference:

$$d \sin \theta = m\lambda$$

where:

d is the distance between the slits

θ is the angle from the central bright fringe

m is the order of the fringe (m = 0 is the central fringe, m = 1 is the first bright fringe on either side, etc.)

λ is the wavelength of the light

Intensity of the interference pattern:

$I = I0 \, (\sin \beta)^2$

where:

I is the intensity at a given point in the interference pattern

I0 is the intensity of the incident light

$\beta = 2\pi a \sin \theta / \lambda$

a is the width of each slit

Diffraction

Single-slit diffraction:

$\sin \theta = \lambda / a$

where:

θ is the angle from the central bright fringe

λ is the wavelength of the light

a is the width of the slit

Intensity of the single-slit diffraction pattern:

$I = I0 \, (\sin \beta)^2$

where:

I is the intensity at a given point in the diffraction pattern

I0 is the intensity of the incident light

$\beta = \pi a \sin \theta / \lambda$

Double-slit diffraction:

$d \sin \theta = m\lambda$

where:

d is the distance between the slits

θ is the angle from the central bright fringe

m is the order of the fringe

λ is the wavelength of the light

Intensity of the double-slit diffraction pattern:

$I = I0 (\sin \beta)^2$

where:

I is the intensity at a given point in the diffraction pattern

I0 is the intensity of the incident light

$\beta = (m\pi a + \pi d) / \lambda$

a is the width of each slit

d is the distance between the slits

formulas related to standing waves:

General formulas:

The equation for a standing wave is:

$$y(x,t) = A \sin(kx - \omega t + \phi)$$

where:

$y(x,t)$ is the displacement of the medium at position x and time t

A is the amplitude of the wave

k is the wave number

ω is the angular frequency

ϕ is the phase constant

The wavelength of a standing wave is related to its wave number by the following formula:

$$\lambda = 2\pi/k$$

The frequency of a standing wave is related to its angular frequency by the following formula:

$$f = \omega/2\pi$$

The speed of a standing wave is equal to the speed of the traveling waves that interfere to create it. This can be calculated using the following formula:

$$v = \omega/k$$

Formulas for standing waves on a string with two fixed ends:

The possible wavelengths of a standing wave on a string with two fixed ends are given by the following formula:

$$\lambda = 2L/n$$

where:

L is the length of the string

n is a positive integer

The frequencies of the possible standing waves are given by the following formula:

$$f = nv/2L$$

where:

v is the speed of the wave on the string

Formulas for standing waves in air:

The possible wavelengths of a standing wave in air are given by the following formula:

$$\lambda = 4L/n$$

where:

L is the distance between the two boundaries that reflect the wave

n is a positive integer

The frequencies of the possible standing waves are given by the following formula:

$$f = nv/4L$$

where:

v is the speed of sound in air

formulas related to polarization:

Brewster's angle

Brewster's angle is the angle of incidence at which light is completely polarized after reflection from a dielectric surface. It is given by the following formula:

$$\tan \theta_B = n2 / n1$$

where:

θ_B is Brewster's angle

n1 is the refractive index of the medium in which the light is incident

n2 is the refractive index of the medium in which the light is reflected

Malus' law

Malus' law describes the intensity of light after passing through a polarizer. It is given by the following formula:

$$I = I_O \cos^2 \theta$$

where:

I is the intensity of the light after passing through the polarizer

I_O is the intensity of the incident light

θ is the angle between the direction of polarization of the incident light and the axis of the polarizer

Degree of polarization

The degree of polarization of light is a measure of how much the light is polarized. It is given by the following formula:

$$P = (I\_max - I\_min) / (I\_max + I\_min)$$

where:

P is the degree of polarization

I_{max} is the intensity of the light when the axis of the polarizer is aligned with the direction of polarization of the light

I_{min} is the intensity of the light when the axis of the polarizer is perpendicular to the direction of polarization of the light

Polarization by double refraction

Double refraction is a phenomenon in which light is split into two beams when it passes through certain materials. This can be used to polarize light. The angle between the two beams is given by the following formula:

$$\delta = 2\,\pi\,d\,(n_e - n_o) / \lambda$$

where:

δ is the angle between the two beams

d is the thickness of the material

n_e and n_o are the refractive indices of the material for extraordinary and ordinary light, respectively

λ is the wavelength of the light

Polarization by diffraction

Diffraction can also be used to polarize light. The intensity of the diffracted light depends on the polarization of the incident light. The following formula can be used to calculate the intensity of the diffracted light:

$$I = I_0 \cos^2 \theta$$

where:

I is the intensity of the diffracted light

I_0 is the intensity of the incident light

θ is the angle between the direction of polarization of the incident light and the plane of diffraction

46. formulas related to electrostatics:

Coulomb's law:

$$F = k * q1 * q2 / r^2$$

where:

F is the force between two point charges

k is Coulomb's constant, approximately equal to 9.0×10^9 Nm^2/C^2

q1 and q2 are the charges of the two point charges

r is the distance between the two point charges

Electric field:

$$E = F / q$$

where:

E is the electric field at a point

F is the force on a unit charge at that point

q is the unit charge

Electric potential:

$$V = k * q / r$$

where:

V is the electric potential at a point

k is Coulomb's constant

q is the charge creating the electric potential

r is the distance from the charge to the point

Capacitance:

$$C = Q / V$$

where:

C is the capacitance of a capacitor

Q is the charge on the capacitor

V is the voltage across the capacitor

Gauss's law:

$$\oint E \cdot dA = Q / \varepsilon_0$$

where:

$\oint E \cdot dA$ is the integral of the electric field over a closed surface

Q is the net charge enclosed by the surface

ε_0 is the permittivity of free space

Electric dipole moment:

$$p = q * d$$

where:

p is the electric dipole moment

q is the magnitude of the charge

d is the distance between the charges

Electric field of a dipole:

$$E = k * p * \cos(\theta) / r^3$$

where:

E is the electric field at a point

k is Coulomb's constant

p is the electric dipole moment

θ is the angle between the dipole moment and the position vector to the point

r is the distance from the dipole to the point

Torque on a dipole in an electric field:

$$\tau = p \times E$$

where:

τ is the torque on the dipole

p is the electric dipole moment

E is the electric field

Potential energy of a dipole in an electric field:

$$U = -p \cdot E$$

where:

U is the potential energy of the dipole

p is the electric dipole moment

E is the electric field

47. formulas related to current electricity:

Electric current:

$$I = tQ$$

$$I = nAv_qd$$

where:

I is the electric current in amperes (A)

Q is the charge in coulombs (C)

t is the time in seconds (s)

n is the number of charge carriers per unit volume

A is the cross-sectional area of the conductor in square meters (m^2)

v_d is the drift velocity of the charge carriers in meters per second (m/s)

Voltage:

$$V = QE$$

$$V = IR$$

where:

V is the voltage in volts (V)

E is the electric potential energy in joules (J)

R is the resistance in ohms (Ω)

Resistance:

$$R = A\rho l$$

$$R = IV$$

where:

ρ is the resistivity of the conductor in ohm-meters (Ωm)

l is the length of the conductor in meters (m)

Power:

$P=IV$

$P=I2R$

$P=RV2$

where:

P is the power in watts (W)

Kirchhoff's laws:

Junction rule: The algebraic sum of all currents at a junction is zero.

Loop rule: The algebraic sum of all voltages around a closed loop is zero.

48. formulas related to the magnetic effects of current:

Force on a current-carrying wire in a magnetic field:

$F = BIl \sin(theta)$

where:

F is the force in Newtons

B is the magnetic field strength in Teslas

I is the current in Amperes

L is the length of the wire in meters

theta is the angle between the wire and the magnetic field

Magnetic field strength due to a current-carrying wire:

$$B = \mu_0 I / 2\pi r$$

where:

B is the magnetic field strength in Teslas

μ_0 is the permeability of free space ($4\pi \times 10^{-7}$ T· m· A-1)

I is the current in Amperes

r is the distance from the wire in meters

Magnetic field strength due to a solenoid:

$$B = \mu_0 n I$$

where:

B is the magnetic field strength in Teslas

μ_0 is the permeability of free space ($4\pi \times 10^{-7}$ T· m· A-1)

n is the number of turns per meter

I is the current in Amperes

Magnetic field strength due to a toroid:

$$B = \mu_0 n I / 2\pi r$$

where:

B is the magnetic field strength in Teslas

μ0 is the permeability of free space ($4\pi \times 10{-7}$ T· m· A-1)

n is the number of turns

I is the current in Amperes

r is the radius of the toroid in meters

Torque on a current loop in a magnetic field:

$$\tau = NIAB \sin(theta)$$

where:

τ is the torque in Newton-meters

N is the number of turns in the loop

I is the current in Amperes

A is the area of the loop in square meters

B is the magnetic field strength in Teslas

theta is the angle between the loop and the magnetic field

formulas related to magnetism:

Magnetic force between two point poles:

$$F = k * m1 * m2 / r^2$$

where:

F is the magnetic force in newtons (N)

k is the Coulomb constant, equal to approximately 9.0×10^9 N m^2/C^2 m1 and m2 are the magnetic moments of the two poles in ampere-meters squared (Am^2)

r is the distance between the two poles in meters (m)

Magnetic field strength at a distance r from a point pole:

$$B = k * m / r^2$$

where:

B is the magnetic field strength in teslas (T)

k is the Coulomb constant

m is the magnetic moment of the pole in Am^2

r is the distance from the pole in m

Magnetic field strength inside a solenoid:

$$B = \mu O * n * I$$

where:

B is the magnetic field strength in T

μO is the permeability of free space, equal to approximately 4π x 10^-7 T m/A

n is the number of turns of wire per meter in the solenoid

I is the current flowing through the solenoid in amperes (A)

Magnetic force on a current-carrying wire:

$$F = B * I * L$$

where:

F is the magnetic force in N

B is the magnetic field strength in T

I is the current flowing through the wire in A

L is the length of the wire in m

Magnetic flux through a surface:

$$\Phi = B * A * \cos(\theta)$$

where:

Φ is the magnetic flux in webers (Wb)

B is the magnetic field strength in T

A is the area of the surface in square meters (m^2)

θ is the angle between the magnetic field and the surface normal

Faraday's law of induction:

$$\varepsilon = -d\Phi/dt$$

where:

ε is the induced electromotive force (EMF) in volts (V)

Φ is the magnetic flux in Wb

t is the time in seconds (s)

Lenz's law:

formulas related to electromagnetic induction:

Faraday's law of induction:

$$\varepsilon = -d\Phi/dt$$

where:

ε is the induced electromotive force (EMF) in volts (V)

Φ is the magnetic flux in webers (Wb)

t is the time in seconds (s)

This law states that the induced EMF in a circuit is equal to the negative rate of change of magnetic flux through the circuit.

Lenz's law:

The direction of the induced EMF is such that it opposes the change in magnetic flux that produced it.

Motional EMF:

$$\varepsilon = Blv$$

where:

ε is the motional EMF in volts (V)

B is the magnetic field strength in teslas (T)

l is the length of the conductor in meters (m)

v is the velocity of the conductor in meters per second (m/s)

This formula describes the EMF induced in a conductor moving through a magnetic field.

Self-inductance:

$$L = \Phi/I$$

where:

L is the self-inductance in henries (H)

Φ is the magnetic flux linked with the circuit in webers (Wb)

I is the current in the circuit in amperes (A)

Self-inductance is a property of a circuit that opposes changes in current through the circuit.

Mutual inductance:

$$M = \Phi_{12}/I_1$$

where:

M is the mutual inductance in henries (H)

Φ_{12} is the magnetic flux linked with circuit 1 due to the current in circuit 2 in webers (Wb)

I_1 is the current in circuit 1 in amperes (A)

Mutual inductance is a property of two circuits that causes an EMF to be induced in one circuit due to a change in current in the other circuit.

Energy stored in a magnetic field:

$$U = 1/2LI^2$$

where:

U is the energy stored in the magnetic field in joules (J)

L is the self-inductance in henries (H)

I is the current in the circuit in amperes (A)

This formula describes the energy stored in the magnetic field of a circuit.

formulas related to alternating current (AC):

Peak voltage: The maximum voltage of an AC waveform.

Peak current: The maximum current of an AC waveform.

Average voltage: The average value of the voltage over a complete cycle.

Average current: The average value of the current over a complete cycle.

RMS voltage: The root mean square voltage of an AC waveform. The RMS voltage is value of a DC voltage that would produce the same heating effect as the AC voltage.

RMS current: The root mean square current of an AC waveform. The RMS current is value of a DC current that would produce the same heating effect as the AC current.

Frequency: The number of cycles of an AC waveform per second. Frequency is measured in Hertz (Hz).

Period: The time it takes for one complete cycle of an AC waveform. Period is measured in seconds (s).

Phase angle: The difference in phase between two AC waveforms. Phase angle is measured in degrees (°).

Impedance: The total opposition to current flow in an AC circuit. Impedance is measured in ohms (Ω).

Resistance: The opposition to current flow due to the material of a conductor. Resistance is measured in ohms (Ω).

Inductive reactance: The opposition to current flow due to the inductance of a circuit. Inductive reactance is measured in ohms (Ω).

Capacitive reactance: The opposition to current flow due to the capacitance of a circuit. Capacitive reactance is measured in ohms (Ω).

Ohm's law for AC circuits:

$$V = IZ$$

where:

V is the voltage in volts (V)

I is the current in amperes (A)

Z is the impedance in ohms (Ω)

Power in AC circuits:

$$P = VI$$

where:

P is the power in watts (W)

V is the voltage in volts (V)

I is the current in amperes (A)

Resonance in AC circuits:

A circuit is in resonance when the inductive reactance and capacitive reactance are equal. At resonance, the impedance of the circuit is at a minimum and the current is at a maximum.

Power factor in AC circuits:

The power factor of an AC circuit is the ratio of the real power (P) to the apparent power (S). The apparent power is the product of the voltage and current.

$$\text{Power factor} = P / S = \cos(\phi)$$

where:

ϕ is the phase angle between the voltage and current

A power factor of 1 indicates that the circuit is purely resistive. A power factor of 0 indicates that the circuit is purely inductive or capacitive.

formulas related to alternating current (AC) generators and transformers:

AC Generator Formulas

Frequency: $f = 1 / T$, where f is the frequency in hertz and T is the period in seconds.

Voltage: $V = E * \sin(2 * pi * f * t)$, where V is the voltage in volts, E is the peak voltage in volts, f is the frequency in hertz, and t is the time in seconds.

Current: $I = I\_m * \sin(2 * pi * f * t + phi)$, where, I_m is peak current, f is the frequency in hertz, t is the time in seconds, and phi is the phase angle in radians.

Power: $P = V * I$, where P is the power in watts, V is the voltage in volts, and I is the current in amps.

Transformer Formulas

Turns ratio: $N\_p / N\_s = V\_p / V\_s$, where N_p is the number of primary turns, N_s is the number of secondary turns, V_p is the primary voltage, and V_s is the secondary voltage.

Current ratio: $I\_p / I\_s = N\_s / N\_p$, where I_p is the primary current, I_s is the secondary current, N_s is the number of secondary turns, and N_p is the number of primary turns.

Power: $P\_p = P\_s$, where P_p is the primary power and P_s is the secondary power.

formulas related to alternating current (AC) circuits:

Voltage: $V = I * Z$

Current: $I = V / Z$

Impedance: $Z = \sqrt{(R^2 + (Xl - Xc)^2)}$

Resistance: $R = V / I$

Inductive reactance: $Xl = 2 * \pi * f * L$

Capacitive reactance: $Xc = 1 / (2 * \pi * f * C)$

where:

V is the voltage in volts (V)

I is the current in amperes (A)

Z is the impedance in ohms (Ω)

R is the resistance in ohms (Ω)

Xl is the inductive reactance in ohms (Ω)

Xc is the capacitive reactance in ohms (Ω)

f is the frequency in hertz (Hz)

L is the inductance in henries (H)

C is the capacitance in farads (F)

some additional formulas related to AC circuits:

Power factor: $PF = \cos(\theta) = R / Z$

Apparent power: $S = V * I$

Real power: $P = V * I * \cos(\theta)$

Reactive power: $Q = V * I * \sin(\theta)$

where:

PF is the power factor

θ is the phase angle

S is the apparent power in voltamperes (VA)

P is the real power in watts (W)

Q is the reactive power in voltamperes reactive (VAR)

formulas related to LCR circuits:

Impedance: Impedance is the total opposition to current flow in an LCR circuit. It is a combination of resistance, inductance, and capacitance. Its formula is given by:

$$Z = \sqrt{R^2 + (XL - XC)^2}$$

where:

Z is the impedance in ohms

R is the resistance in ohms

XL is the inductive reactance in ohms

XC is the capacitive reactance in ohms

Inductive reactance: Inductive reactance is the opposition to current flow in an inductor. It is given by the formula:

$$XL = 2\pi fL$$

where:

XL is the inductive reactance in ohms

f is the frequency in hertz

L is the inductance in henries

Capacitive reactance: Capacitive reactance is the opposition to current flow in a capacitor. It is given by the formula:

$$XC = 1/(2\pi fC)$$

where:

XC is the capacitive reactance in ohms

f is the frequency in hertz

C is the capacitance in farads

Quality factor: The quality factor of an LCR circuit is a measure of its selectivity. It is given by the formula:

$$Q = Z/(XL - XC)$$

where:

Q is the quality factor

Z is the impedance in ohms

XL is the inductive reactance in ohms

XC is the capacitive reactance in ohms

Resonant frequency: The resonant frequency of an LCR circuit is the frequency at which the inductive reactance and capacitive reactance are equal. It is given by the formula:

$$f\_r = 1/(2\pi\sqrt{(LC)})$$

where:

f_r is the resonant frequency in hertz

L is the inductance in henries

C is the capacitance in farads

Bandwidth: The bandwidth of an LCR circuit is the range of frequencies over which the impedance is within 70.7% of its resonant impedance. It is given by the formula:

$$BW = f\_r/Q$$

where:

BW is the bandwidth in hertz

f_r is the resonant frequency in hertz

Q is the quality factor

formulas related to electromagnetic waves:

Speed of light in a vacuum:

$$c = 299,792,458 \text{ m/s}$$

Wavelength and frequency:

$$f = c / \lambda$$

where:

f is the frequency in hertz (Hz)

c is the speed of light in a vacuum in meters per second (m/s)

λ is the wavelength in meters (m)

Energy of a photon:

$$E = hf$$

where:

E is the energy of the photon in joules (J)

h is Planck's constant, which is equal to 6.626×10^{-34} J $\cdot$ s

f is the frequency of the photon in hertz (Hz)

Intensity of an electromagnetic wave:

$$I = P / A$$

where:

I is the intensity in watts per square meter (W/m²)

P is the power in watts (W)

A is the area in square meters (m²)

Reflection and refraction:

Snell's law: $\sin(\theta_1) / \sin(\theta_2) = v_1 / v_2$

where:

θ_1 is the angle of incidence

θ_2 is the angle of refraction

v_1 is the speed of the wave in the first medium

v_2 is the speed of the wave in the second medium

Diffraction:

Single slit diffraction: $d \sin(\theta) = \lambda$

where:

d is the width of the slit

θ is the angle of diffraction

λ is the wavelength of the wave

Polarization:

Malus' law: $I = I_0 \cos^2(\theta)$

where:

I is the intensity of the transmitted light

I0 is the intensity of the incident light

θ is the angle between the polarization of the incident light and the polarization axis of the analyzer

formulas related to ray optics:

Reflection

Law of reflection: the angle of incidence is equal to the angle of reflection.

Refraction

Snell's law: $n_1 \sin \theta_1 = n_2 \sin \theta_2$, where n_1 and n_2 are the refractive indices and θ_1 and θ_2 are the angles of incidence and refraction, respectively.

Critical angle: the angle of incidence at which the angle of refraction is 90°.

Total internal reflection: occurs when light is incident on a denser medium from a rarer medium at an angle greater than the critical angle.

Lenses

Lens maker's formula: $1/f = (n - 1)(1/R_1 - 1/R_2)$, where f is the focal length of the lens, n is the refractive index of the lens material, and R_1 and R_2 are the radii of curvature of the two lens surfaces.

Lens equation: $1/v - 1/u = 1/f$, where u is the object distance, v is the image distance, and f is the focal length of the lens.

Magnification: $m = v/u$, where m is the magnification of the lens.

Optical instruments

Simple microscope: $m = D/f$, where m is the magnification of the microscope, D is the distance between the object and the eyepiece, and f is the focal length of the objective lens.

Compound microscope: $m = m_o \times m_e$, m_o is the magnification of the objective lens, and m_e is the magnification of the eyepiece.

Astronomical telescope: $m = -f_o/f_e$, where m is the magnification of the telescope, f_o is the focal length of the objective lens, and f_e is the focal length of the eyepiece.

57. formulas related to optical instruments:

Mirror formula:

$$1/f = 1/u + 1/v$$

where:

f is the focal length of the mirror

u is the object distance

v is the image distance

Magnification of a mirror:

$$m = -v/u$$

where:

m is the magnification

v is the image distance

u is the object distance

Lens maker's formula:

$$1/f = (n - 1) * (1/R1 - 1/R2)$$

where:

f is the focal length of the lens

n is the refractive index of the lens material

R1 is the radius of curvature of the first surface of the lens

R2 is the radius of curvature of the second surface of the lens

Lens formula:

$$1/v - 1/u = 1/f$$

where:

v is the image distance

u is the object distance

f is the focal length of the lens

Magnification of a lens:

$$m = v/u$$

where:

m is the magnification

v is the image distance

u is the object distance

Simple microscope:

$$m = D/f$$

where:

m is the magnification

D is the distance between the object and the lens

f is the focal length of the lens

Compound microscope:

$$m = M_o * M_e$$

where:

m is the overall magnification

M_o is the magnification of the objective lens

M_e is the magnification of the eyepiece lens

Astronomical telescope:

$$m = -f_o / f_e$$

where:

m is the magnification

f_o is the focal length of the objective lens

f_e is the focal length of the eyepiece lens

Resolving power of a telescope:

$$R = 1.22 * lambda / D$$

where:

R is the resolving power

lambda is the wavelength of light

D is the diameter of the objective lens

Wave Optics Formulas:

Wave Equation

$$v = \lambda f = \omega / k$$

where:

v is the wave velocity

λ is the wavelength

f is the frequency

ω is the angular frequency

k is the wavenumber

Superposition Principle

$$y = y_1 + y_2 + y_3 + \ldots$$

where:

y is the resultant displacement at a point due to multiple waves

$y_1, y_2, y_3, \ldots$ are the displacements at that point due to each individual wave

Young's Double Slit Experiment

$$d \sin \theta = m\lambda$$

where:

d is the distance between the slits

θ is the angle between the central maximum and the mth order bright fringe

m is the order of the bright fringe

λ is the wavelength of light

Diffraction Grating

$$d \sin \theta = n\lambda$$

where:

d is the grating constant

θ is the angle between the central maximum and the nth order bright fringe

n is the order of the bright fringe

λ is the wavelength of light

Polarization

$$I = I0 \cos^2 \theta$$

where:

I is the intensity of transmitted light

$I0$ is the intensity of incident light

θ is the angle between the planes of polarization of the incident and transmitted light

Brewster's Law

$$\tan \theta p = \mu 2 / \mu 1$$

where:

θp is the polarizing angle

$\mu 1$ is the refractive index of the incident medium

$\mu 2$ is the refractive index of the refracted medium

Total Internal Reflection

$$\sin \theta c = 1 / \mu$$

where:

θc is the critical angle

μ is the refractive index of the denser medium

58.formulas related to the dual nature of matter and radiation:

De Broglie wavelength:

$$\lambda = h / p$$

where:

λ is the wavelength

h is Planck's constant

p is the momentum

This formula shows that all particles have a wavelength, which is determined by their momentum.

Energy of a photon:

$$E = hf$$

where:

E is the energy of the photon

h is Planck's constant

f is the frequency of the photon

This formula shows that photons have both wave and particle properties. As waves, they have a frequency and wavelength. As particles, they have an energy.

Photoelectric effect:

$$KE\_max = hf - \phi$$

where:

KE_max is the maximum kinetic energy of the photoelectrons

h is Planck's constant

f is the frequency of the incident light

Φ is the work function of the metal

This formula shows that the maximum kinetic energy of the photoelectrons is determined by the frequency of the incident light and the work function of the metal. The work function is the minimum energy required to remove an electron from the metal.

Compton effect:

$$\lambda' = \lambda + h \,/\, mc(1 - \cos\theta)$$

where:

λ' is the wavelength of the scattered photon

λ is the wavelength of the incident photon

h is Planck's constant

m is the mass of the electron

c is the speed of light

θ is the scattering angle

This formula shows that the wavelength of a photon is changed when it scatters off an electron. The change in wavelength is determined by the scattering angle and the mass of the electron.

59. formulas related to matter waves:

De Broglie wavelength:

$$\lambda = h/p$$

where:

λ is the wavelength of the matter wave

h is Planck's constant

p is the momentum of the particle

Relationship between energy and frequency:

$$E = hf$$

where:

E is the energy of the particle

f is the frequency of the matter wave

Relationship between wavelength and momentum:

$$p = h/\lambda$$

Relationship between wavelength and energy:

$$\lambda = h/\sqrt{2mE}$$

where:

m is the mass of the particle

Davisson-Germer experiment:

$$d \sin\theta = n\lambda$$

where:

d is the distance between the slits

θ is the scattering angle

n is an integer

De Broglie wavelength of electrons:

$$\lambda = h/(2mqeV)^{\frac{1}{2}}$$

where:

q is the charge of the electron

V is the accelerating voltage

m is the mass of the electron

formulas related to atomic structure:

Atomic Number

Atomic number = Number of protons = Number of electrons

Mass Number

Mass number = Number of protons + Number of neutrons

Number of Neutrons

Number of neutrons = Mass number – Atomic number

Radius of the Nucleus

Radius of the nucleus = 1.2 x 10^-15 meters x A^(1/3)

where A is the mass number

Energy of the Photon

Energy of the photon = hc/λ

where h is Planck's constant, c is the speed of light, and λ is the wavelength of the photon

Photoelectric Effect

$$KE = hc/\lambda - \phi$$

where KE is the kinetic energy of the ejected photoelectron, ϕ is the work function of the metal surface, and λ is the wavelength of the incident photon

Bohr's Model for Hydrogen and Hydrogen-like Ions

Quantization of Angular Momentum

$$mvr = nh/2\pi$$

where m is the mass of the electron, v is the velocity of the electron, r is the radius of the electron's orbit, n is the principal quantum number, and h is Planck's constant

Energy Levels

$$E_n = -E_1/n^2$$

where En is the energy of the electron in the nth energy level, E1 is the energy of the electron in the ground state, and n is the principal quantum number

Radius of the Electron's Orbit

$$r_n = n^2h^2/4\pi^2me^2$$

where rn is the radius of the electron's orbit in the nth energy level, h is Planck's constant, π is the mathematical constant pi, me is the mass of the electron, and e is the charge of the electron

Velocity of the Electron

$$v_n = 2\pi ze^2/nh$$

where vn is the velocity of the electron in the nth energy level, z is the atomic number, e is the charge of the electron, h is Planck's constant, and n is the principal quantum number

Ionization Energy

Ionization energy = Energy required to remove an electron from an atom

Electron Affinity

Electron affinity = Energy released when an electron is added to an atom

Excitation Energy

Excitation energy = Energy required to move an electron from a lower energy level to a higher energy level

De-Excitation Energy

De-excitation energy = Energy released when an electron moves from a higher energy level to a lower energy level

Number of Spectral Lines

Number of spectral lines = $(n_2 - n_1 + 1)(n_2 - n_1)/2$

where n_2 is the higher energy level and n_1 is the lower energy level

Schrodinger Wave Equation

$$H\psi = E\psi$$

where H is the Hamiltonian operator, ψ is the wave function, and E is the energy

Total Number of Nodes

Total number of nodes = $n - 1$

where n is the principal quantum number

61. formulas related to radioactivity:

Half-life: The half-life of a radioactive isotope is the time it takes for half of the atoms in a sample to decay. It can be calculated using the following formula:

$$t\_h = \ln(2)/\lambda$$

where:

th is the half-life in seconds

λ is the decay constant in seconds^-1

Activity: The activity of a radioactive sample is the number of decays per second. It can be calculated using the following formula:

$$A = \lambda N$$

where:

A is the activity in decays per second

λ is the decay constant in seconds^-1

N is the number of atoms in the sample

Decay constant: The decay constant is a measure of how quickly a radioactive isotope decays. It is defined as the probability of decay per unit time. It can be calculated using the following formula:

$$\lambda = \ln(2)/t\_h$$

where:

λ is the decay constant in seconds^-1

th is the half-life in seconds

Decay rate: The decay rate is the change in the number of radioactive atoms in a sample over time. It can be calculated using the following formula:

$$R = -dN/dt$$

where:

R is the decay rate in decays per second

N is the number of radioactive atoms in the sample

t is the time in seconds

Specific activity: The specific activity of a radioactive substance is the activity per unit mass. It can be calculated using the following formula:

$$a = A/m$$

where:

a is the specific activity in decays per second per gram

A is the activity in decays per second

m is the mass of the sample in grams

Nuclear energy is the energy released from the nucleus of an atom. It can be released in two main ways: nuclear fission and nuclear fusion.

Nuclear fission is the process of splitting a heavy nucleus into two lighter nuclei. This process releases a large amount of energy, as well as neutrons. The neutrons can then be used to split other nuclei, creating a chain reaction.

Nuclear fusion is the process of combining two light nuclei to form a heavier nucleus. This process also releases a large amount of energy.

Einstein's mass-energy equivalence formula is the fundamental formula for nuclear energy:

$$E = mc^2$$

where:

E is energy in joules

m is mass in kilograms

c is the speed of light in a vacuum (299,792,458 meters per second)

This formula shows that mass and energy are equivalent and can be converted into each other. The small amount of mass that is converted into energy in nuclear reactions is what gives nuclear energy its tremendous power.

Other important formulas related to nuclear energy include:

Binding energy: The binding energy of a nucleus is the energy required to separate all of the nucleons in the nucleus. It is also equal to the energy released when the nucleons come together to form the nucleus.

Mass defect: The mass defect of a nucleus is the difference between the mass of the individual nucleons and the mass of the nucleus itself. It is equal to the mass that is converted into energy when the nucleus forms.

Nuclear fission chain reaction: A nuclear fission chain reaction is a process in which neutrons released from the fission of one nucleus cause the fission of other nuclei, releasing more neutrons, and so on. This process can continue until all of the fissile material is consumed.

Nuclear fusion reaction: A nuclear fusion reaction is a process in which two light nuclei combine to form a heavier nucleus, releasing energy. The most common nuclear fusion reaction is the fusion of two hydrogen nuclei to form a helium nucleus.

Examples of how the above formulas are used in nuclear energy applications:

Calculating the energy released in a nuclear fission reaction:

Energy released = (mass of reactants – mass of products) * c^2

For example, the fission of one uranium-235 nucleus releases about 200 MeV of energy.

Calculating the binding energy of a nucleus:

Binding energy = (mass of individual nucleons - mass of nucleus) * c^2

For example, the binding energy of a helium-4 nucleus is about 28.3 MeV.

Calculating the number of neutrons produced in a nuclear fission reaction:

Number of neutrons produced = number of neutrons in reactants - number of neutrons in products

For example, the fission of one uranium-235 nucleus produces about 2.5 neutrons.

Calculating the energy required to initiate a nuclear fusion reaction:

Energy required = (mass of products - mass of reactants) * c^2

For example, the fusion of two hydrogen nuclei to form a helium nucleus requires about 5.5 MeV of energy.

62.Formulas related to semiconductors

Intrinsic semiconductors

Intrinsic carrier concentration:

n_i = sqrt(Nc * Nv) * exp(-Eg / 2kT)

where:

n_i is the intrinsic carrier concentration (cm-3)

Nc is the effective density of states in the conduction band (cm-3)

Nv is the effective density of states in the valence band (cm-3)

Eg is the bandgap energy (eV)

k is Boltzmann's constant (eV/K)

T is the temperature (K)

Doping

Doping concentration:

$$N_a = N_d = N$$

where:

N_a is the acceptor concentration (cm-3)

N_d is the donor concentration (cm-3)

N is the doping concentration (cm-3)

Electrical conductivity

Electrical conductivity:

$$\sigma = n_e \mu_e + n_h \mu_h$$

where:

σ is the electrical conductivity (Ω-1cm-1)

n_e is the electron concentration (cm-3)

μ_e is the electron mobility (cm2/Vs)

n_h is the hole concentration (cm-3)

μ_h is the hole mobility (cm2/Vs)

p-n junction

Built-in potential:

$$V_{bi} = (kT/q) * \ln(n_i{}^2 / n_e * n_h)$$

where:

Vbi is the built-in potential (V)

k is Boltzmann's constant (eV/K)

T is the temperature (K)

q is the elementary charge (1.602×10^{-19} C)

ni is the intrinsic carrier concentration (cm^{-3})

ne is the electron concentration in the n-region (cm^{-3})

nh is the hole concentration in the p-region (cm^{-3})

Depletion width:

$$W = sqrt(2\varepsilon sVbi / q(ne + nh))$$

where:

W is the depletion width (cm)

εs is the semiconductor permittivity (F/cm)

Vbi is the built-in potential (V)

q is the elementary charge (1.602×10^{-19} C)

ne is the electron concentration in the n-region (cm^{-3})

nh is the hole concentration in the p-region (cm^{-3})

Forward current:

$$If = I0 (exp(qV / kT) - 1)$$

where:

If is the forward current (A)

I0 is the reverse saturation current (A)

q is the elementary charge (1.602 x 10-19 C)

V is the forward voltage (V)

k is Boltzmann's constant (eV/K)

T is the temperature (K)

Reverse curren

Ir = I0

where:

Ir is the reverse current (A)
I0 is the reverse saturation current (A)

Transistors

Common base current gain:

α = ΔIC / ΔIE

where:

α is the common base current gain

ΔIC is the change in collector current (A)

ΔIE is the change in emitter current (A)

Common emitter current gain:

$$\beta = \Delta IC / \Delta IB$$

where:

β is the common emitter current gain

ΔIC is the change in collector current (A)

ΔIB is the change in base current (A)

Common collector current gain:

$$\gamma = \Delta IE / \Delta IB = \beta + 1$$

where:

γ is the common collector current gain

ΔIE is the change in emitter current (A)

ΔIB is the change in base current (A)

63.formulas related to semiconductor diodes:

Diode current-voltage relationship:

$$I = I_s(e^{V/V_T} - 1)$$

where:

I is the diode current

Is is the diode saturation current

V is the diode voltage

VT is the thermal voltage (approximately 26 mV at room temperature)

Diode forward voltage drop:

$$V_f = V_T \ln(I/I_s + 1)$$

where:

Vf is the diode forward voltage drop

I is the diode current

Is is the diode saturation current

VT is the thermal voltage (approximately 26 mV at room temperature)

Diode reverse voltage breakdown:

$$V_b = V_z + V_d$$

where:

Vb is the diode reverse voltage breakdown

Vz is the diode zener voltage

Vd is the diode dynamic breakdown voltage

Diode junction capacitance:

$$C_j = C_{jo}(1 - V/V_{bi})^{-m}$$

where:

Cj is the diode junction capacitance

Cjo is the diode junction capacitance at zero bias

V is the diode voltage

Vbi is the diode built-in potential

m is a diode parameter typically between 0.3 and 0.5

Diode dynamic resistance:

$r\_d = V\_T/I$

where:

rd is the diode dynamic resistance

VT is the thermal voltage (approximately 26 mV at room temperature)

I is the diode current

formulas related to the seven basic logic gates:

AND gate:

Output = A * B

where A and B are the inputs to the AND gate.

OR gate:

Output = A + B

where A and B are the inputs to the OR gate.

NOT gate:

Output = !A

where A is the input to the NOT gate.

NAND gate:

$$Output = !(A * B)$$

where A and B are the inputs to the NAND gate.

NOR gate:

$$Output = !(A + B)$$

where A and B are the inputs to the NOR gate.

XOR gate:

$$Output = A * !B + !A * B$$

where A and B are the inputs to the XOR gate.

XNOR gate:

$$Output = !(A * !B + !A * B)$$

where A and B are the inputs to the XNOR gate.

Here are some examples of how to use the formulas:

To design a circuit to turn on a light if either switch A or switch B is pressed, you would use an OR gate. The output of the OR gate would be connected to the lightbulb.

To design a circuit to turn on a light only if both switch A and switch B are pressed, you would use an AND gate. The output of the AND gate would be connected to the lightbulb.

To design a circuit to turn on a light if switch A is pressed but not switch B, you would use an XOR gate. The output of the XOR gate would be connected to the lightbulb.

The formulas for logic gates can also be used to solve Boolean algebra problems. For example, to solve the problem "A AND (NOT B)", you would use the following formula:

$$A\ AND\ (NOT\ B) = A * !B$$

This formula tells us that the output of the circuit will be true only if A is true and B is false.

formulas related to transistors:

Current gain (β): The current gain of a transistor is the ratio of the collector current to the base current. It is also known as the forward current transfer ratio (hfe).

$$\beta = Ic / Ib$$

Voltage gain (Av): The voltage gain of a transistor is the ratio of the output voltage to the input voltage. It is also known as the forward voltage gain (hfe).

$$Av = Vout / Vin$$

Input resistance (Rin): The input resistance of a transistor is the resistance seen at the base terminal. It is also known as the small-signal input resistance.

$$Rin = Vbe / Ib$$

Output resistance (Rout): The output resistance of a transistor is the resistance seen at the collector terminal. It is also known as the small-signal output resistance.

$$Rout = Vce / Ic$$

Transconductance (gm): The transconductance of a transistor is the change in collector current per unit change in base current. It is also known as the small-signal transconductance.

$$gm = Ic / Vbe$$

Cut-off frequency (fc): The cut-off frequency of a transistor is the frequency at which the current gain drops to unity. It is also known as the transition frequency (ft).

$$fc = ft / \beta$$

formulas related to transistors:

Power dissipation (Pd): The power dissipation of a transistor is the maximum power that can be dissipated without causing the transistor to overheat.

$$Pd = Ic * Vce$$

Efficiency (η): The efficiency of a transistor is the ratio of the output power to the input power.

$$\eta = Pout / Pin$$

Gain-bandwidth product (GBP): The gain-bandwidth product of a transistor is the product of the gain and the bandwidth. It is a measure of the transistor's ability to amplify high-frequency signals.

$$GBP = Av * fc$$

formulas related to communication systems:

The Shannon-Hartley theorem: This theorem states that the maximum rate of transmission of information over a noisy channel is equal to the bandwidth of the channel times the logarithm to the base two of one plus the signal-to-noise ratio.

The Nyquist-Shannon sampling theorem: This theorem states that a signal must be sampled at a rate at least twice the highest frequency component of the signal in order to be perfectly reconstructed.

The Fourier transform: This mathematical transform converts a signal from the time domain to the frequency domain.

The inverse Fourier transform: This mathematical transform converts a signal from the frequency domain to the time domain.

The convolution operation: This operation combines two signals to produce a third signal.

The correlation operation: This operation measures the similarity between two signals.

In addition to these general formulas, there are also many formulas specific to different types of communication systems. For example, in a digital communication system, the following formulas are commonly used:

The bit error rate (BER): This is the probability of a bit being received incorrectly.

The frame error rate (FER): This is the probability of a frame being received incorrectly.

The packet error rate (PER): This is the probability of a packet being received incorrectly.

The signal-to-noise ratio (SNR): This is the ratio of the power of the signal to the power of the noise.

The channel capacity: This is the maximum rate at which information can be transmitted over a channel without error.

In an analog communication system, the following formulas are commonly used:

The bandwidth: This is the range of frequencies that a signal occupies.

The modulation index: This is the ratio of the change in the carrier frequency to the maximum change in the carrier frequency.

The noise figure: This is a measure of the quality of a receiver.

The dynamic range: This is the difference between the strongest and weakest signals that a receiver can detect.

formulas related to amplitude modulation (AM):

Modulated signal:

$$y(t) = A_c(1 + \mu \cos(2\pi f_m t))\cos(2\pi f_c t)$$

where:

$y(t)$ is the modulated signal

A_c is the amplitude of the carrier signal

μ is the modulation index

f_m is the frequency of the modulating signal

f_c is the frequency of the carrier signal

t is time

Modulation index:

$$\mu = A_m / A_c$$

where:

μ is the modulation index

Am is the amplitude of the modulating signal

Ac is the amplitude of the carrier signal

Percentage of modulation:

$$\%M = \mu * 100$$

where:

%M is the percentage of modulation

μ is the modulation index

Bandwidth of an AM signal:

$$BW = 2fm$$

where:

BW is the bandwidth of the AM signal

fm is the frequency of the modulating signal

Power of an AM signal:

$$P = P\_c + P\_usb + P\_lsb$$

where:

P is the total power of the AM signal

P_c is the power of the carrier signal

P_usb is the power of the upper sideband

P_lsb is the power of the lower sideband

Single-sideband (SSB) AM:

$$y(t) = Ac(1 + \mu cos(2\pi fmt))cos(2\pi fct + \phi)$$

where:

$y(t)$ is the SSB AM signal

Ac is the amplitude of the carrier signal

μ is the modulation index

fm is the frequency of the modulating signal

fc is the frequency of the carrier signal

ϕ is the phase shift

t is time

Double-sideband suppressed-carrier (DSB-SC) AM:

$$y(t) = Ac\mu cos(2\pi fmt)cos(2\pi fct)$$

where:

$y(t)$ is the DSB-SC AM signal

Ac is the amplitude of the carrier signal

μ is the modulation index

fm is the frequency of the modulating signal

fc is the frequency of the carrier signal

t is time

Formulas related to radio waves:

Speed of radio waves

$$v = \lambda f$$

where:

v is the speed of the radio wave in meters per second (m/s)

λ is the wavelength of the radio wave in meters (m)

f is the frequency of the radio wave in hertz (Hz)

Frequency of radio waves

$$f = v / \lambda$$

Wavelength of radio waves

$$\lambda = v / f$$

Energy density of radio waves

$$u = \varepsilon_0 \, E^2 / 2 = B^2 / 2\mu_0$$

where:

u is the energy density of the radio wave in joules per cubic meter (J/m³)

ε_0 is the permittivity of free space in farads per meter (F/m)

E is the electric field strength of the radio wave in volts per meter (V/m)

B is the magnetic field strength of the radio wave in teslas (T)

μ_0 is the permeability of free space in henrys per meter (H/m)

Intensity of radio waves

$$I = c \left| E \times B \right|$$

where:

I is the intensity of the radio wave in watts per square meter (W/m²)

c is the speed of light in vacuum in meters per second (m/s)

Radio wave power

$$P = IA$$

where:

P is the power of the radio wave in watts (W)

A is the area of the surface receiving the radio wave in square meters (m²)

Radio wave attenuation

$$A = e^{(-\alpha x)}$$

where:

A is the ratio of the transmitted radio wave power to the received radio wave power

e is the base of the natural logarithm

α is the attenuation coefficient in nepers per meter (Np/m)

x is the distance between the transmitter and receiver in meters (m)

Formulas related to receiving and detecting radio waves:

Radio wave propagation:

Radio wave equation: This equation describes the power of a radio wave at a distance from the source antenna:

$$P\_r = P\_t * G\_t * G\_r * lambda^2 / (4 * pi * d^2 * L)$$

where:

Pr   is the power received at the receiving antenna (in watts)

Pt   is the power transmitted at the transmitting antenna (in watts)

Gt   is the gain of the transmitting antenna

Gr   is the gain of the receiving antenna

λ is the wavelength of the radio wave (in meters)

d is the distance between the transmitting and receiving antennas (in meters)

L is the loss factor (due to atmospheric absorption, etc.)

Friis transmission formula: This is a simplified version of the radio wave equation that can be used for free space propagation:

$$P\_r = P\_t * G\_t * G\_r * lambda^2 / (4 * pi * d^2)$$

where the loss factor is assumed to be 1.

Radio wave reception:

Antenna impedance: The impedance of an antenna is a measure of its resistance to the flow of current. It is important to match the impedance of the antenna to the impedance of the receiver in order to maximize power transfer.

$$Z\_a = R\_a + j * X\_a$$

where:

Za   is the antenna impedance (in ohms)

Ra   is the antenna resistance (in ohms)

Xa   is the antenna reactance (in ohms)

Receiver sensitivity: The receiver sensitivity is the minimum signal power that the receiver can detect. It is typically measured in decibels below 1 microwatt (dBm).

Sensitivity = 10 * log(P_min / 1 µW) dBm

where:

Pm   in is the minimum signal power that the receiver can detect (in watts)

Signal-to-noise ratio (SNR): The SNR is a measure of the ratio of the desired signal power to the noise power. It is important to have a high SNR in order to detect and decode radio signals accurately.

SNR = 10 * log(P_signal / P_noise) dB

where:

Ps   ignal is the desired signal power (in watts)

Pn   oise is the noise power (in watts)

Radio wave detection:

Energy detector: An energy detector is a simple radio wave detector that measures the total power of the received signal. It is not able to distinguish between different types of signals.

Energy = integral(P_r(t), 0, T) dt

where:

Energy is the energy of the received signal (in joules)

Pr   (t) is the received signal power (in watts)

T is the integration time (in seconds)

Matched filter: A matched filter is a more sophisticated radio wave detector that is designed to detect a specific type of signal. It is able to maximize the SNR and improve the detection probability.

Matched Filter Output = y(t) = integral(x(t) * h(t), 0, T) dt

where:

$y(t)$ is the output of the matched filter

$x(t)$ is the received signal

$h(t)$ is the impulse response of the matched filter

<u>Epilouge</u>

As I pen down the final words of this book, "Physics All Formulas Class 11 & 12," I am filled with a sense of accomplishment and gratitude. This journey, which began as an endeavor to simplify and illuminate the world of physics for students, has been a remarkable one.

Throughout these pages, we have delved into the fundamental principles of physics, covering a diverse range of topics that form the cornerstone of your Class 11 and 12 curriculum. From the laws of motion to electromagnetism, from waves to modern physics, we've strived to provide you with a concise, comprehensive, and easily digestible collection of formulas and concepts.

I must acknowledge the invaluable assistance of artificial intelligence in the creation of this book. AI technology has played a pivotal role in organizing, refining, and presenting the wealth of information contained within these pages. It has allowed us to bring you a book that is not only informative but also accessible, making your revision process smoother and more efficient.

The purpose of this book is simple: to serve as a reliable companion in your academic journey. Whether you are preparing for exams, seeking clarification on a specific concept, or simply reviewing the formulas and equations that define the world of physics, I hope this book has been of great help to you.

To the readers, I hope this book has ignited or deepened your passion for physics. Remember that learning is a lifelong journey, and the pursuit of knowledge is a noble endeavor. Keep asking questions, keep exploring, and keep reaching for the stars, for the universe is a vast and wondrous place waiting for you to uncover its secrets.

Thank you for choosing "Physics All Formulas Class 11 & 12" as your guide. I wish you all the success and fulfillment in your physics studies and beyond.

With warm regards,

Md Saif Ali

70 TOPICS INCLUDED
SIMPLE AND ILLUSTRATIVE
BY - MD SAIF ALI
(AI ASSISTED)